PENGUIN BUSINESS

FROM INVISIBLE TO INVALUABLE

Nasir Zaidi is a seasoned corporate leader with over twenty-eight years of experience in banking, specializing in process redesign. A Six Sigma Green Belt and holder of a master's in English and a postgraduate diploma in journalism, he brings a unique blend of technical and creative skills to his writing.

With a social media following of over 1,25,000, Nasir coaches and mentors aspiring professionals. He is a published author (three self-published books and one traditionally published) and an avid reader, writer, traveller and cricket enthusiast. Married to Farhat, a student-success coach, they have two children: Saamish, a doctor in the UK, and Insia, an e-commerce professional in Dubai. Nasir is also a fitness enthusiast, a stock market investor and a former creative writing instructor. He is currently writing a book on motivation.

He was recently appointed to the board of directors at Lushescapes, a leading luxury bespoke travel company.

FROM INVISIBLE TO INVALUABLE

100 GAME-CHANGING STRATEGIES TO EXCEL AT THE WORKPLACE

NASIR ZAIDI

PENGUIN
BUSINESS

An imprint of Penguin Random House

PENGUIN BUSINESS

USA | Canada | UK | Ireland | Australia
New Zealand | India | South Africa | China | Singapore

Penguin Business is an imprint of the Penguin Random House group of companies
whose addresses can be found at global.penguinrandomhouse.com

Published by Penguin Random House India Pvt. Ltd
4th Floor, Capital Tower 1, MG Road,
Gurugram 122 002, Haryana, India

Penguin
Random House
India

First published in Penguin Business by Penguin Random House India 2024

ISBN 9780143471318

Typeset in Garamond by MAP Systems, Bengaluru, India

Printed at Repro India Limited

www.penguin.co.in

MIX
Paper from
responsible sources
FSC® C047271

This is a legitimate digitally printed version of the book and therefore might not
have certain extra finishing on the cover.

For my brother Afsar, who means the world to me

Contents

Forewords

Bright young people entering the professional world put in their best efforts to become successful in their careers. Yet, more often than not, many of them reach a point where their progress becomes sluggish or comes to a complete halt. Many of these young people have arrived at the workplace after enduring the tough competition and gruelling selection process at schools or colleges. But somehow their skills seem inadequate after a point. This situation is evident not just in the context of a job, but also in entrepreneurship or business. We have all come across intelligent and hard-working professionals who toil without reward or recognition while others seem to race ahead. Often when these professionals hit a roadblock, they blame their bosses or investors, their company or the 'system'. They are capable and committed but when success eludes them, they become bitter and frustrated.

If you want to be the professional with the Midas touch and find success in anything you touch and also be a magnet for opportunities and people who will take your career to lofty heights, then you have come to the right place. Nasir Zaidi's book is that treasure trove of wisdom that will not only deliver on this promise but will set you up for much bigger success in life, whether your goal is to pursue a corporate career or make your mark in entrepreneurship.

Nasir has distilled his experience of three decades in the corporate world in India and overseas to come up with this masterpiece. He has understood the fine nuances of human behaviour and the value systems that can lead to sustainable success. This is not a book of success-in-easy-steps or some quick-fix solutions. After all, building a successful career is serious business and there are no shortcuts to it.

I wish you the very best in your journey through this book. I am sure it will set you on the path to a rewarding and successful career.

Deepak Mehra
author of *Ready, Steady, Go!* (2015)
and *Think Like a Golfer, Win Like a Golfer* (2023)

Have you ever met someone who left a lasting impression on your mind? Someone you find yourself remembering and referring to during interesting conversations, perhaps even months and years after you have met them?

Nasir is that someone for me.

We first met virtually for a podcast I was hosting. Nasir had agreed to make time for one of the inaugural episodes, and I was immediately struck by his wisdom, decades-long corporate experience, intriguing perspectives on a wide range of topics and clarity of thought, which together combined into a sparkling cocktail that made for a delightful conversation.

From Invisible to Invaluable is a book that both details and distils the breadth of Nasir's experience into an essential handbook for professionals who would like to survive and thrive in the rapidly changing corporate landscape. From developing resilience amidst difficult environments and shifting your mindset until you can start perceiving challenges as opportunities, to visualizing your way to your goals, *From Invisible to Invaluable* will give you all the tools you need to excel in your current and future roles.

Nasir is one of the most well-read people that I have had the pleasure of meeting. This book blends insights from his reading journeys with his personal learnings to create a comprehensive manual that will let you navigate and craft your own corporate voyage. Written with Nasir's characteristic flair and ability to cut straight to the heart of what's important, you will enjoy reading this book almost as much as you will appreciate the success that applying the principles outlined in the book will get you.

As one of its early readers, I can confidently say that the book has a lot of value to offer and I would strongly recommend *From Invisible to Invaluable* to corporate veterans and beginners alike.

Best of luck, and happy reading!

Mudit Mohilay
entrepreneur, writer and
director of marketing, Encora Inc.

Preface

The idea of writing this book germinated from the work-related reels that I have been posting on my Instagram handle for close to two years now.

Having worked in the corporate world for over twenty-eight years in various capacities, I understand the difficulties and the challenges that employees face every day. Some are because of their own limitations, some because of the limiting policies and procedures of their organizations and some because of a toxic manager or environment.

To write this book, I have heavily relied on my own experiences, on the experiences of professionals I have known, the various books and articles that I have read (at the end of this book, you will find a list of them) and the interactions that I have had with my social media followers.

The workplace is a dynamic ecosystem. Survival is an everyday challenge. To be able to shine in such a place is just a fancy dream for many. The purpose behind this book is to help as many working professionals as possible to create a niche for themselves in their respective work areas.

This book is your road map to unlocking your full potential and shining brightly within your professional sphere. Whether you are a seasoned professional seeking to reignite your passion or a newcomer eager to make a lasting impression, this book offers valuable tools and insights to illuminate your path to success.

In this book, you will find a 100 ways to SHINE at work. Through stories and anecdotes, I have highlighted the significance of each way, then described briefly the way and ended each chapter with action points.

You will get ideas about essential skills, strategic self-branding, confidence building and navigating through complex situations that will help you discover your authentic voice, contribute meaningfully and build a fulfilling career that you can be truly proud of. Hope you shine in your work and life.

1

Improve Productivity

*Productivity is being able to do things that
you were never able to do before.*

—Franz Kafka

Two legendary companies—Microsoft and Apple—were engaged in a tussle to release their operating systems first.

Microsoft took five years and 10,000 employees to do it.

Apple took just two years and 600 employees.

Apple took considerably less time and fewer employees and yet produced a superior product. How did they achieve this?

Both are excellent companies. So how could one do a better job than the other? It was because of the approach that the companies decided to take. While Microsoft rewarded *individual performance*, Apple focused on rewarding *team performance*.

The difference in their approach made all the difference.

Michael Mankins writes in his book, *Time, Talent, Energy*, that 'for every member of the team that is not a star player, productivity declines'.

So, to be a star player, you should be performing at your highest level. Not only should you be efficient at work, but you should also be consistently improving your productivity.

About Improving Productivity

Productivity makes the organization effective. It is a key to its profitability. The more productive the organization is, the more it increases its ability to thrive and become successful.

A highly productive firm can provide an unbelievable client experience, thereby gaining customer loyalty, and a loyal customer is the best ambassador for the business.

When the company does well, based on improved productivity, it can offer incentives to employees in the shape of bonuses and other perks, thus leading to an increase in the overall motivational level.

To thrive in today's competitive landscape, consistent productivity is non-negotiable. Continuous improvement is the only path forward.

Do not confuse productivity with capability. Capability is the power or ability to do something. Productivity is the efficiency with which tasks are performed by you. You can be very capable without being productive enough. To be classified as a star performer, you should be both capable and productive. Growth in productivity does not happen automatically.

If you wish to go up the corporate ladder, you need to focus on improving your productivity. Self-confidence, a positive attitude, a sense of commitment, willingness to explore outside the comfort zone and the ability to know which task to tackle first will help you to increase your productivity.

Action Points

Manage tasks strategically:

1. Prioritize.
2. Schedule.
3. Minimize distractions.

Utilize time effectively:

1. Batch similar tasks together.
2. Use time management tools like Microsoft To Do, Google Calendar, Toggl Track, etc.

Set Goals and delegate:

1. Break down large projects into smaller milestones.
2. Identify areas for improvement.
3. Wherever possible, delegate.

Remember,

Strategic action is the catalyst for productivity breakthroughs.

2

Be a Problem-Solver

There's no use talking about the problem
unless you talk about the solution.

—Betty Williams

What would you do if you were asked to bring home something to *eat*, *drink*, *plant in the garden* and *feed the cows* using just one coin?

This task was assigned by a merchant to his son. The son was baffled by the work given to him. He went from one place to another seeking a solution to this problem but was unable to find it. Until he met a girl with whom he fell in love. When he shared the problem with her, she gave him a watermelon.

Surprised, he wondered how watermelon could be the solution? But when she told him, he felt a surge of excitement.

He came home with the watermelon and cut it into two halves and gave one portion to his father to *eat*, then he cut the middle pink flesh and extracted juice from it and gave part of it to his father to *drink*, then he collected the watermelon seeds to *plant in the garden* and kept the green, hard peels to *feed the cows*.

The moral of this story is that a difficult problem could very well have a simple solution.

About Being a Problem-solver

At every workplace, there is a surfeit of problems. Don't add to those problems. You can be a force to reckon with if you develop yourself as a problem-solver. So be a seeker of solutions.

You can become a problem-solver only if you stop being rigid in your thinking. Vertical thinking limits possibilities. Use the lateral thinking technique. This approach is without the limitations imposed by logic-based critical thinking.

Some more ideas to help you become an expert problem-solver:

- Use 5 Why analysis.
- Take a contrarian view.
- Consider the worst-case scenario.
- Reconstruct the problem.
- Use 'What-If' analysis.

You can also try another effective problem-solving method called the Problem Approach Method, described by M.R. Kopmeyer in his book *Thoughts to Build On*.

- Write down exactly what the problem is.
- Write down exactly what are the causes of the problem.
- Write down every possible effective solution.
- Decide definitely which solution to put into effect.
- Start immediately to put that solution into effect.

There are many more problem-solving methods, but that is beside the point. The point is to be a problem-solver, not a problem-maker.

Action Points

Develop a structured approach:

1. Define (the problem)
2. Analyse (the problem)
3. Develop (solutions)
4. Evaluate (solutions)
5. Select (solution)
6. Implement (solution)
7. Measure (outcome)

Hone your analytical skills:

1. Evaluate solutions objectively.
2. Consider different perspectives (take opinions/views of people who are not from your department or background).
3. Critically examine the proposed solution.

Practise regularly:

1. Seek out opportunities to practice problem-solving skills in various situations.
2. Solve puzzles and riddles.
3. Turn daily challenges into opportunities, for example, consider an appliance malfunction as a chance to troubleshoot.

Remember,

Simple Instructions + Right Tools = Problem Solved.

3

Embrace the Unknown

How can you know what you're capable of
if you don't embrace the unknown?
—Esmeralda Santiago

Once upon a time there was a frog by the name of Finn who lived at the bottom of a well. This well was the whole world for Finn. He had never ventured out of the well and had spent his entire life in the comfort of this world.

Then one day, the well ran dry. In order to survive, Finn decided to hop out of the well to see what he could of the end of the world. With a trembling heart, he peered out. What the hell is this, he thought? There's a whole new world outside my world, he said.

Enchanted, enthralled, excited, he ventured out of his world to explore this brand new world.

Aren't we all like Finn?

Living in our wells and thinking that this is all there is.

If we continue to be narrow-minded, we will become stagnant. The only way to broaden our horizons is to shun our narrow-mindedness.

About Embracing the Unknown:

Nothing ventured, nothing gained. Yes, the Unknown inspires fear. But if you remain inert, this fear will overwhelm you and you will become inept and incapable of handling any stuff outside your area of work.

Doing just your work, fulfilling your responsibilities alone, will, at the most, make you a 'meets all expectations' employee. You will be just one among many. To stand apart, you must embrace the unknown.

Explore the possibility of doing something that you haven't done before. Grab the opportunities that scare you. Learn, ask, research, put in effort, do whatever it takes, but show your manager that you can manage tasks that you have no prior experience of.

If you play safe, you will be entrenched in one place. You may think you are secure, but you will not gain or learn anything. Becoming stagnant is the worst thing you can do to yourself as a person and as a professional.

Success isn't supposed to happen, no matter how hard you work. There's no guarantee you're going to succeed. There's nothing set in stone.

Fear of failure can be a career-killer. By clinging to the familiar, you risk being left behind.

Take small steps. Test the waters by seeking controlled risks and as you taste success, take the plunge. By diving headlong into the sea of uncertainty, you will emerge as a new you. Go ahead, dither not. By embracing the unknown, you will enrich your life and career.

Action Points

Be open to experiences:

1. Embrace new hobbies.
2. Meet new people.
3. Consume diverse media on topics outside your usual interests.

Activate your imagination:

1. Engage your senses.
2. Play mind games.
3. Learn a new skill.

Develop intellectual curiosity:

1. Keep a journal.
2. Challenge your existing beliefs.
3. Travel.

Remember,

Our own learning limits us.

4

Be Intentional

Your intentions create your reality.

—Wayne Dyer

Intention is the compass that guides us to our destination. This story of a determined ninety-two-year-old woman is a prime example. En route to witness her grandson's academic triumph, she found herself unexpectedly stranded in the heart of Utah. With graduation day rapidly approaching and no immediate flight options, most would have crumbled. Not her. Her unwavering commitment to her grandson would ignite a spark that would illuminate her path forward.

As she kept mulling over how she would reach Idaho on time for the event, she overheard a conversation between two men sitting close to her. One of them, who appeared to be in his late forties, was saying that he had to be in Idaho for his son's graduation by 7 a.m. on Saturday.

Without a moment's hesitation, she approached the gentleman and said, 'I too have to reach Idaho for my grandson's graduation.'

Such is the power of intentionality, that in less than an hour, two complete strangers—fuelled by a common purpose—had teamed up and rented a car. And soon they were on the road from Salt Lake City to Idaho and by 5.30 a.m. on Saturday, they had reached their destination.

About Being Intentional:

Do not wait for things to happen. Be like that ninety-two-year-old grandmother. Do not wait to see what's going to happen next. That's a reactive state and it won't lead you anywhere.

You want that sale deal to close. Make it happen.

You want that project to be a success. Make it happen.

You want people to listen to you. Make it happen.

You want that issue to be fixed. Make it happen.

Just sitting idle and hoping for something to happen is like living in a fool's paradise. 'Create what you desire,' says mindset coach Maki Moussavi in her book, *The High Achiever's Guide*, 'by deliberate thought and actions.'

So, don't waste time in brooding, overthinking and getting upset and frustrated. If things aren't working in your favour, be intentional and make magic happen. If you wait to respond after something happens, your wait will never end.

To advance your career, align your choices with your aspirations by defining your goals, developing your vision, prioritizing your values and creating a strategic plan.

Understand that being intentional is akin to decluttering your mind. Not everything is a priority. You can become intentional by being purposeful and deliberate in all your actions.

Decide how you want to act. Don't let external forces decide for you.

Action Points

Align actions with priorities:

1. Have a clear vision for the day/week/month/year/life.
2. Say 'No' if the task or request clashes with your priorities.
3. Set aside time for what matters the most.

Practise self-awareness:

1. Know your strengths and weaknesses.
2. Engage in activities that promote mindfulness like meditation, deep breathing.
3. Sharpen your focus.

Learn from setbacks:

1. Don't dwell on failures.
2. Analyse what went wrong.
3. Identify the areas for improvement and adjust your approach moving forward.

Remember,

Intentional choices are deliberate and purposeful decisions.

5

Think Progress, Not Perfection

Perfection is a roadblock to progress.

—Unknown

Do you remember the race to fly between the Wright brothers, who ran a bicycle shop, and the wealthy US government, with a budget of $2 million?

Whose plane would take off first?

The US government thought only of perfection. A plane ought to fly straight or it will crash. Zero imperfections was their goal.

The Wright brothers also had similar thoughts until they saw a boy learning to ride a bicycle. The boy wobbled at first, before taking off. The brothers changed their perspective. Instead of focusing on perfection, they focused on progress. They made a plane that wobbled and flew, creating history.

They were able to pip the US government with its millions only because they had the vision to realize that life is about progress, not perfection.

About Thinking Progress, Not Perfection:

Perfection is stagnancy. Progress is growth. Remember, we are born to make mistakes. Mistakes are bound to happen. Don't let the fear of making mistakes cripple you from moving forward. Shift your focus from being perfect to making progress.

Learn from your mistakes. Making mistakes is not a problem. Making the same mistake is foolishness. Adapt to new situations and seek newer ways to succeed.

Don't confuse progress with negligence. Striving for perfection can be paralyzing. As Sheryl Sandberg said, 'done is better than perfect'. Focus on moving forward, not on achieving unattainable ideals.

Be like the seed that grows into a tree without bothering about perfection. It just keeps growing, keeps progressing.

The bridge that connects your ability with your ambition is progress. Ignore the big drama. Just focus on the next step. Grow, improve, develop, that's what progress means. When we strive for perfection, we become critical and judgemental about ourselves and others. Be a person of action. Not a robot of perfection.

Action Points

Mindset shift:

1. Celebrate small wins.
2. Embrace the learning process.
3. Analyse failures from different angles.

Be compassionate to yourself:

1. Acknowledge limitations.

2. Make yourself ready for positive quitting (when you are sure that you have given the task/assignment the best you could, but it is not leading to what you are hoping for).
3. Accept self-doubt, instead of fighting it.

Ignore the chatter of your mind:

1. Practice relaxation techniques.
2. Explore meditation apps like Headspace and Calm, among others.
3. Challenge negative thought patterns that contribute to mind chatter.

Remember,

Perfection is an illusion.

6

Add Value

*You become a star not because of your title; you become
a star because you are adding star value to your company.*

—N.R. Narayana Murthy

Rajat Sharma was a model assistant manager. Ambitious and hardworking, he yearned for the next step up the corporate ladder. Two consecutive promotions denied, he sought answers from his boss.

'Rajat, what unique value do you bring to the table?' she inquired.

Stunned, he detailed his duties.

She smiled, 'That's your job, Rajat. I'm looking for your exceptional contribution, not your routine.'

About Adding Value:

The logic is simple.

The more you 'bring to the table', the more visible you become in the organization. When you are more visible, you attract more opportunities. When you get more opportunities, you can give a boost to your career.

Also, when times get tough, you will be more secure than others because you will have built a reputation for yourself as someone who adds value.

You can add value to your organization by focusing on tasks and assignments that can lead to:

- increase in revenue
- reduction in cost
- development of your personal brand

Once you add value, you increase your worth to your organization and become more indispensable. Master a skill and let it be known to all that you are an expert in a specific area. Know what's happening around you and within your industry.

Also, consistency is important. You cannot be known as someone who adds value if you do it only once or a couple of times. You must do it regularly. Every day, seek to add value to someone or something. Make it a habit. Make 'add value' your middle name.

Action Points

Deliver high-quality work:

1. Don't miss deadlines.
2. Produce exceptional results.
3. Exceed expectations consistently.

Be proactive:

1. Identify inefficiencies.
2. Anticipate potential challenges.
3. Take initiative and ownership.

Go the extra mile:

1. Do stuff that is over and above your core responsibilities.
2. Do, without being asked; be a go-getter.
3. Highlight your achievements.

Remember,

> By being good at something, you become valuable.
> By adding value, you become indispensable.

7

Take Intelligent Risks

The biggest risk is not taking any risk.
—Mark Zuckerberg

The mid-90s was an era of banking metamorphosis. I was a cog in the operational machinery of a Mumbai bank as it embarked on this transformative journey. The introduction of a sales department, a radical departure for the institution, was met with trepidation by most. Yet, a flicker of ambition ignited within me. With no sales experience to my name, I volunteered. This audacious step was the catalyst for unprecedented professional growth.

Fast forward several years to the Middle East. As a seasoned retail banker, I was presented with an unexpected challenge: to helm the branch's operations. The decision was fraught with uncertainty. To abandon the familiar for the unknown was a risky proposition. But history had taught me the power of calculated risks. Once again, I stepped outside my comfort zone, and once again, it proved to be a pivotal moment in my career.

About Taking Intelligent Risks:

The first question that will arise in your mind is *why should I take risks?* The second question that will trouble you is *what if I fail?* And finally, you will brood over *why should I put my job and reputation in jeopardy?* These are normal questions.

We are not comfortable with failure. We forget that success is nothing but a series of failures. At the same time, we should also understand that taking risks does not mean being reckless. Recklessness is a sure remedy for disaster.

There is a difference between rash risks and intelligent risks. We should be smart enough to take intelligent risks. Of course, there is no guarantee that intelligent risks will work. But you are assured that there won't be any catastrophe.

Some examples of intelligent risks are:

- initiating a new project
- accepting a task that others are reluctant to do (after understanding why they are reluctant)
- accepting a new role
- challenging the ways in which work is done
- taking extra responsibility
- doing a task that is outside your work experience
- changing your career path

If you don't take risks, you stunt your growth. Eliminate FPPIC—Fear, Perfection, Procrastination, Irrationality and Codependence. All these are obstacles in the path of taking intelligent risks.

Action Points

Do calculated assessment and planning:

1. Identify what you want to do and why.
2. Understand what the consequences would be if you went ahead or if you didn't.
3. Assess the worst-case scenario.

Leverage knowledge and expertise:

1. Consult individuals who have successfully navigated similar risks in the past.
2. Conduct pilot tests or simulations.
3. Evaluate the results.

Set clear boundaries:

1. Establish predefined risk tolerance.
2. Take calculated risks in less consequential areas.
3. Understand the risk landscape and potential outcomes.

Remember,

Intelligent risks are calculated leaps, while recklessness is a blind plunge. The former opens doors to endless possibilities, while the latter jeopardizes everything.

8

Don't Gossip

Gossip is the Devil's radio.

—George Harrison

Here's a poem by Oliya Charkhi that I found on the internet.

Once I tarnish a reputation it is never the same
The wound I inflict never heals
I overthrow governments and ruin marriages
I destroy careers and cause sleepless nights
I generate suspicion and grief
I make innocent people cry
My name hisses hate
Yes, my name is Gossip

About Not Gossiping:

Workplace gossip can have a negative impact. So beware. Do not indulge in gossip or encourage it in any way.

Nancy Kurland and Lisa Pelled in their article 'Passing the Word: Toward a Model of Gossip and Power in the Workplace,' which appeared in the April 2000 issue of *Academy of Management Review*, have listed these negative consequences of workplace gossip:

- Erosion of trust and morale
- Loss of productivity and wasted time
- Increased anxiety among employees as rumours circulate without clear information as to what is a and isn't a fact
- Divisiveness among employees as people take sides
- Hurt feelings and reputations
- Attrition due to good employees leaving the company, because of an unhealthy work environment

There's not much to gain through gossip, except some moments of false bliss, but there is so much to lose, as highlighted by Kurland and Pelled.

Why put one's reputation at stake?

Trust gets eroded. Teamwork gets hindered. The work atmosphere gets polluted. All this combined together affects the productivity of the team. Gossip may appear harmless, but it isn't.

By saying no to gossip, you give a clear signal that you mean business at work. Colleagues will respect you more for taking such a stand.

Action Points

Be mindful of your words:

1. Take a moment to consider the consequences of your words before sharing any information about others.
2. Ask yourself before sharing anything if you would want the same to be shared about you.
3. Share only objective observations and avoid subjective interpretations or judgements.

Redirect the conversation:

1. Change the subject when gossip starts.
2. Move away by excusing yourself if gossip continues.
3. Engage in discussions about neutral subjects.

Establish limits:

1. Ignore those who gossip; stay away from them.
2. Do not talk about your private life.
3. Express your discomfort.

Remember,

The more you dwell on others, the less significant
you become.

9

Be a Team Player

Teamwork makes the dream work.

—John Maxwell

Steve Wynn, the founder of Wynn Resort and Casino, narrates an interesting story about his family's vacation in Paris. It is a perfect example of teamwork.

They were staying at the Four Seasons Hotel. Wynn had ordered breakfast in the room. His daughter took a few bites of a croissant and left half of it for later. The family then left for sightseeing.

On their return to the hotel room, the daughter was disappointed on seeing that her croissant was gone. She thought housekeeping had taken it away while cleaning the room.

But to everyone's surprise, there was a message from the front desk on the telephone. It said that the housekeeping employee had got rid of the half-eaten croissant, with the thought that they would prefer a fresh croissant upon their arrival. So front desk had planned with the kitchen to keep one ready and room service had been told to provide it when the request was made.

This was magic. The way different departments had interacted and worked as a cohesive unit to delight the customer was exemplary.

That's what teamwork does. It converts dream into reality.

About Being a Team Player:

You may be a brilliant worker but if you can't work in a team, with a team, for a team and as a team, then your credibility suffers. By being a team player, you demonstrate that you are willing to sacrifice or underplay your individual brilliance for the sake of the team's success. You will shine more if you have this attitude.

Be receptive to your team members' ideas. Those ideas may not be doable. But by encouraging team members to come forward and share their ideas, you will be able to inculcate camaraderie and team spirit within the team.

As a team player, you will have to exhibit flexibility on many occasions. For instance, your manager may ask you to do something that you are not so confident about or tell you to assist a junior in their assignment. Do not become angry or panicky; accept whatever comes your way.

In a cricket match, the skipper prefers players who keep the interests of the team first, instead of focusing on their own accomplishments. The captain may tell a key player that he will need to sit out a match for various reasons. Take the example of R. Ashwin. A great player by any stretch of the imagination. But time and again, the team management has left him out of matches, and he has taken it sportingly.

Help, listen, communicate, respect, solve, celebrate. That's how you become an effective team player. For better outcomes, promoting a positive work environment and enhanced creativity and productivity, being a team player is essential.

Action Points

Collaborate:

1. Understand the team's objectives.
2. Share information.
3. Support and be supported.

Have a proactive mindset:

1. Maintain a positive attitude.
2. Listen to different perspectives.
3. Consider alternative approaches.

Celebrate achievements and focus on the team:

1. Reinforce a sense of collective accomplishment.
2. Give more weightage to the team's goals, rather than to individual recognition.
3. Commemorate the smallest milestones.

Remember,

Individually we may not be that effective,
but collectively, as a team, we can achieve the impossible.

10

Exude Positivity

Whatever your mind can conceive and believe, it can achieve.
—Napoleon Hill

A poor man saved every penny he could for twenty years. With the amount that he accumulated, he built a house for his family. Everyone was delighted. An auspicious date was chosen to shift to the new house.

But two days before the move, a massive earthquake struck. The poor man's house was reduced to rubble and debris. The entire neighbourhood felt sad for the poor man. Some shook their heads in disbelief. Some were heartbroken. Some even cried inconsolably.

The poor man, on the other hand, was happy and distributed sweets to everyone. No one could understand this behaviour. One of them asked, 'What's wrong with you? Your house has been destroyed, and you are celebrating.'

The poor man replied, 'You are seeing only the negative side. But I am seeing the positive side. Imagine what would have happened if this earthquake had struck two days later, when my family and I would have been living in it. We would all have perished.'

With this kind of positive outlook towards life, one can do wonders.

About Exuding Positivity:

Positivity is the cornerstone between triumph and defeat. Negativity is a pervasive force, especially in the workplace. Yet, your outlook can be your greatest asset. Radiate optimism and watch as opportunities flock to you. A positive mindset is a catalyst for achievement, transforming obstacles into stepping stones. Cultivate positivity in thought, word and deed, and become a beacon of inspiration to those around you.

Mind your language at all times. Here are a few examples:
Change
'Why not?' to 'Sounds good'.
'No problem' to 'Definitely'.
'I don't have time' to 'I will find time'.
'I don't know' to 'I will learn'.

Mind your body language at all times. Here are a few examples:
Change
A frown to a smile.
Avoiding eye contact to maintaining eye contact.
A limp handshake to a firm handshake.
Arms crossed to open hands with palms facing up.

Mind your feelings at all times. Here are a few examples:
Instead of being:
Anxious, be comfortable.

Frustrated, be satisfied.
Stressed, be enthusiastic.

The more positivity you bring to work, the more positive and enjoyable the environment becomes.

Action Points

Shift your perspective:

1. Focus on the good in people and situations.
2. Reframe negative thoughts.
3. Express gratitude always, and especially, when you think things are not going your way.

Draw a line:

1. Avoid negative people if you can't focus on what's good in them.
2. Train yourself to use only positive language.
3. Appreciate, instead of criticizing.

Take care of yourself:

1. Visualize happiness.
2. Balance work–life.
3. Be physically active.

Remember,

Life is a rollercoaster. The winners are those
who don't let the dips define their journey.

11

See the Big Picture

Understanding the 'big picture' allows you to recognize how elements fit together.

Zayn and his friends were relaxing by the river. The tranquility was shattered by an infant's desperate cry. A tiny life drifted helplessly downstream, a chilling precursor to a nightmare unfolding before their eyes. Moments later another infant floated by, then another.

Too stunned to react, the group realized that if no immediate action was taken, all the babies would drown. One by one, the group plunged into the turbulent waters, a desperate rescue mission in full swing.

Yet, amidst the chaos, Zayn moved in the opposite direction. A chorus of disbelief erupted as he retreated from the drowning infants. Undeterred, he explained, 'I'm stopping this madness at its source.'

About Seeing the Big Picture:

John Maxwell in his book *The 17 Indisputable Laws of Teamwork* writes, 'Your place on the team makes sense only in the context of the big picture.' Often this vital point gets ignored and employees get busy trying to prove their individual performance.

What's the point if you shine but the team fails? Make the team shine. That's what you are there for. That's what the others are there for. That's what we are all there for. Right from the CEO to the lowly clerk. Everyone should aim to help their team to succeed, which will lead to the success of the company. No one's role is too big or too small.

As John Milton said, 'They also serve who only stand and wait'.

Getting used to developing big picture thinking will make you a strategist. Your superiors will appreciate this quality in you. If you can prove to them that you are a 'big picture type' of employee, you can rise quickly in the organization.

Seeing the big picture provides clarity, purpose, self-fulfilment and better results for the company. Ultimately, accomplishing the mission is the goal. Losing a battle or two is okay, if you win the war. Look beyond your immediate sphere of influence and understand how your actions and decisions impact other stakeholders and the organization. When you recognize that what you are doing is interconnected with the larger system, the BIG PICTURE, then you will be able to take actions and decisions that align with the company's long-term goals and values.

Technology is reshaping our world at breakneck speed. To thrive, not just survive, requires a forward-thinking mindset. Equip yourself with the ability to see the bigger picture. It's not just about keeping up; it's about leading the charge.

Action Points

Create a broad perspective:

1. Focus on the outcome (how the project will end), rather than overthinking every step.
2. Look for relationships and interdependencies between isolated events or missing information.
3. Combat confirmation bias by gathering diverse viewpoints.

Develop a holistic understanding:

1. Break/divide large problems into smaller, more manageable components.
2. Don't get bogged down in the immediate details, consider the long-term view.
3. Connect the dots by focusing on the interconnectedness.

Step outside your zone of security:

1. Create ideas using mind mapping techniques.
2. Abandon perfectionism and preconceived notions.
3. Explore unfamiliar territories.

Remember,

Unplug to upgrade your perspective.

12

Question Best Practices

Be disruptive in your approach and don't fall into the trap of doing something in a particular fashion, just because others do it that way— think next practices, not best practices . . . best practices maintain the status quo and next practices shatter it.

—Mike Myatt

Lakhanpal, a fresh face on the factory floor, watched as experienced hands moved in robotic precision. Yet, his observant mind saw beyond the mechanical ballet. While others replicated actions with robotic precision, he noticed the subtle inefficiencies, the silent whispers of a system yearning for optimization. A critical breakdown offered him a chance to illuminate the shadows. His suggestion, born of intuition and observation, was met with skepticism, but it was the spark that ignited a revolution.

Rahman Shaikh, the seasoned supervisor, initially resistant to change, was forced to acknowledge the potency of Lakhanpal's insight. As word of his triumph spread, a collective shift began. The factory floor, once a static landscape, transformed into a fertile ground for innovation. Employees, emboldened by Lakhanpal's courage, started questioning the unquestionable.

The once rigid 'best practices' evolved into dynamic strategies, tailored to the ever-changing demands of the industry.

This story is a testament to the power of human ingenuity when freed from the shackles of conformity. It's a reminder that every system, no matter how complex or established, harbours opportunities for improvement. The key lies in the courage to challenge the status quo and the wisdom to nurture a culture of innovation.

About Questioning Best Practices:

To make a huge difference to the organization you are working for and to enhance your personal brand, start questioning the best practices.

Best practices hamper the organization's growth. They help in maintaining the status quo, but don't enable progress. Unless you develop the ability to question everything that you are doing, you are not going to achieve much for yourself or for the organization.

When you decide to target best practices, your intention should not be to make fun of them or scoff at those who introduced or formulated them. They are best practices for a reason. When they were devised, at that time, they were supposedly the best, but now, in the present moment, they may not be serving the purpose with the same impact and effect.

Best practices can stifle innovation. They make us lazy. We know we are following the best practices so what more there is to do? That's the thought process we develop. But we should be innovating and not replicating.

Trends, technologies, techniques and customer preferences keep changing. But one can surely learn to keep pace with those changes. Therefore, questioning best practices is vitally important. A whole new perspective can emerge by doing so.

As Mike Myatt put it, think *next practices*. That's the way forward. That's the way to progress. So challenge the best practices and innovate new practices.

Action Points

Cultivate a critical mindset:

1. Seek evidence-based reasoning.
2. Consider best practices as the starting point and not the goal.
3. Challenge assumptions.

Foster open communication and inquiry:

1. Delve deeper and ask insightful questions like what's the purpose of this practice? Why can't we do it in a different way? Is this in the best interest of our clients or employees?
2. Engage in constructive dialogue.
3. Encourage a culture of continuous improvement.

Conduct research:

1. Stay informed about industry trends.
2. Analyse how leading companies approach similar challenges.
3. Evaluate the effectiveness of existing practices.

Remember,

Purpose is constant, but practice shouldn't be,
so consider evolving continuously.

13

Take Ownership

Ownership is not a vice, not something to be ashamed of,
but rather a commitment, and an instrument by which
the general good can be served.

—Vaclav Havel

An old mason was ready to retire. He approached his employer–contractor and told him about his plan to leave the house building work and go back to his native village and spend the remainder of his life in a leisurely manner.

The employer–contractor was sorry to lose a good employee. He requested him to build just one more house as a personal favour. The elderly mason could not refuse because of the bond they shared.

He started constructing the house, but he did not do it with his usual meticulousness. His heart was not in the job. So his workmanship was substandard. He completed the task because he felt obliged to. The house looked shoddy and unattractive.

He informed his employer who came to inspect the house and bid his fine worker goodbye. He said nothing to the mason about the quality of his work, but just handed the front door key to him with the words, 'This is your house, a small gift from me.'

The old mason couldn't believe what he had done. If only he had taken ownership of the task given to him, he would have built a fantastic house for himself.

That's what happens when we do not take ownership for the work that we are doing.

About Taking Ownership:

Your manager has appointed you as the leader of a project. You work hard to complete it with your team. You and the team put in extra hours to ensure that the deadline is met. But certain deliverables don't reach you on time. Let's say, the IT department was unable to provide you the requirement, because of which you missed the deadline.

Your manager is upset because of this failed commitment. Your failure means he or she has also failed. Your manager sends for you, and you go ready with your explanation. You know that it is not your fault. The IT department is the culprit. So, the moment the manager asks, 'Why did the project not meet the deadline?' You say, 'I have nothing to do with this. IT did not give us the requirement.'

This is unprofessional. No manager will accept this. What you are doing is rejecting ownership and giving an excuse. The right thing to do in this case is to take ownership (you are the project leader, and the manager manages you, not the IT department), accept the failure of missing the deadline and then explain why it happened. And assure the manager that you are following up with the IT department and soon the matter will be fixed. Such an approach will favour you.

To build trust with your manager, increase your self-confidence and self-worth, and excel in your career, start taking ownership. There's no substitute for it.

As John Miller says in his book *QBQ!* 'Fix the problem, don't affix the blame.' Accept responsibility and focus on finding solutions to problems, instead of looking for excuses.

Action Points

Take initiative and assume responsibility:

1. Don't wait to be assigned tasks. Identify areas for improvement and propose solutions.
2. Be proactive, not reactive.
3. Develop a robust working relationship with your seniors.

Independent problem-solving and action:

1. Identify and analyse challenges.
2. Develop and implement solutions.
3. Monitor progress and adapt as needed.

Communicate and collaborate:

1. Blend your ideas with those of other people, so it's a win-win situation for everyone involved.
2. Keep stakeholders informed about the progress of your work; highlight any challenges or roadblocks.
3. Be open to constructive criticism.

Remember,

By taking ownership, you become a catalyst for change.

14

Do Difficult Things

All things are difficult before they are easy.
—Thomas Fuller

Given two options, most of us usually opt for the easier one. But, by picking the one which is more challenging, we can make a huge difference in our lives.

Conquering discomfort and challenging ourselves equips us to navigate life's uncertainties with confidence.

Michael Phelps, a titan of the pool, clocked sixteen-hour training marathons. Kobe Bryant's basketball court was his monastery, where he logged twelve-hour daily penitence. Thomas Edison's laboratory was a crucible, where a thousand failures were stepping stones to a single incandescent triumph.

These are not mere anecdotes but testaments to a relentless pursuit of excellence. History is replete with individuals who've traded comfort for greatness. Their legacies are a stark reminder: extraordinary achievements are the outcome of doing difficult things.

Pushing through difficulties elevates your potential.

About Doing Difficult Things:

Everyone loves to do the easy stuff. Rare is the individual who will willingly take on a hard task. To set yourself apart from your co-workers, to really make a difference to the team and the organization, to set an example and to dazzle in office, build a reputation for doing difficult things.

Doing difficult things is a strain but if you train yourself to enjoy the journey without worrying too much about the destination, the experience could be life-changing for you. So, say 'yes' to that challenging project that your manager brings up. Accept the tough assignment that no one else will touch.

You must remember one thing though. Taking up the challenging project/tough assignment will benefit you only if you enjoy doing them. You need to love the challenge of doing difficult things. Doing them for the sake of doing them will not produce the desired result. You don't have to give the impression of being a show-off. You must show that you are willing to face the hard challenge, with your high skill.

Psychologist Mihaly Csikszentmihalyi describes the condition of entering this state of high challenge/high skill as *flow*. Once we get into the flow, we fall in love with difficult things. Hard things improve us, sharpen our abilities and prepare us to face uncertainties. Once we form the habit of doing difficult things, we will become so accustomed to the experience that tackling the hard stuff will be like second nature to us.

The mere acceptance of a challenging project/tough assignment will make your manager realize your worth and that, by itself, is a wonderful accomplishment.

Action Points

View challenges as opportunities:

1. Do things that you fear or have been avoiding.
2. Believe that failure only leads to success.
3. Solve numerical puzzles if you are good at words, and word puzzles if numbers are your strength.

Develop resilience:

1. Think of what you will lose by not taking action.
2. Anticipate setbacks and roadblocks.
3. Stay calm when things are not going your way.

Reframe the difficulty:

1. Acknowledge and assess the problem, and work towards finding a solution.
2. Shift your perspective; don't see a problem as a problem, but consider it an opportunity to learn and grow.
3. Explore innovative solutions, instead of simple ones.

Remember,

Patience with small and simple things is essential
for tackling the big and complex things.

15

Respect

If they respect you, respect them. If they disrespect you, still respect them. Do not allow the actions of others to decrease your good manners, because you represent yourself, not others.
—Mohammad Zeyara

Saira's world crumbled under the weight of the manager's single, dismissive phrase: 'Do what I need you to do.' She felt disrespected and a seed of resentment was sown.

Her subsequent acts of defiance, like deliberately misfiling papers, were not merely sabotage but a silent protest against being treated as a cog, not a collaborator. The team suffered as a consequence of a leader's oversight.

Contrast this with the infectious optimism our other manager exuded. His daily affirmations, a sprinkle of human connection amidst the professional grind, ignited a fire within us. We were not just employees; we were valued members of a team. His respect was the kindling, our motivation the flame.

The stark difference between these two styles of leadership underscores an undeniable truth: employees are not merely resources to be exploited; they are individuals deserving of dignity and respect. When treated as such, they respond with loyalty, dedication and a drive to excel.

About Respecting:

Your manners separate you from the herd. The way you communicate, your friendly tone, politeness and humility make others comfortable when they are with you. Be they seniors or juniors, always respect others.

It is not necessary for you to agree with everyone. Agreeing with people has nothing to do with respect. You can disagree with the whole world and yet respect everybody. The point is to not to be impolite, angry, sarcastic, arrogant, hostile or mean to others.

Do not scold, criticize or humiliate anyone. If you aren't happy with the way things are going on in your department or if a team member is being disrespectful, by all means, correct them. But do so without disturbing the harmony. People don't remember titles; they remember their experiences with the people holding those titles.

Be non-judgemental. He is horrid. She is rotten. He is annoying. She is a drama queen. It's not our duty to judge people. Would we like to be labelled as horrid, rotten, annoying or drama queen? Definitely not.

A survey of 20,000 employees by *Harvard Business Review* revealed that respect was the leading behaviour that encourages greater commitment and engagement. So, treat others the way you would like to be treated.

Follow the golden rule taught by Jesus Christ: Do unto others as you would have them do unto you.

Action Points

Promote open communication:

1. Express yourself in easy-to-understand language.
2. Listen carefully; pay close attention to people while they are talking.
3. Be mindful of your tone. Even while disagreeing, use a respectful and professional tone of voice.

Be courteous always:

1. Use appropriate greetings and titles.
2. Avoid invading the personal space of your colleagues.
3. Be punctual and reliable.

Nurture a positive and inclusive work environment:

1. Avoid jokes or humour that could be offensive or hurtful.
2. Do not discuss politics, religion and sex with colleagues.
3. Acknowledge and appreciate the unique contributions of everyone.

Remember,

Treat people with respect; reap the rewards of success.

16

Be an Influential Listener

I remind myself every morning: Nothing I say this day will teach me anything. So, if I'm going to learn, I must do it by listening.
—Larry King

A friend of mine attended an annual day function hosted by his wife's company. He didn't want to go but his wife insisted that everyone would be coming with their spouses and if he didn't go, it would be embarrassing for her. Eventually, he agreed.

On the day of the function, he tried to excuse himself but his wife said that if he didn't go, she wouldn't attend either. Reluctantly, he dressed up, forced a smile and went along with her.

On their way there, he was thinking of what he should say, how he should behave and, most importantly, what he should do to impress his wife's colleagues. When he couldn't make up his mind, he decided that he would only listen to others.

That is exactly what he did. He just listened to people talk. Here and there, he responded with phrases like 'I understand,' or 'I see,' or 'I get your point.' He didn't voice his opinion on any matter and did not utter any other word except for those acknowledgement phrases.

No one realized that he wasn't talking. They were all happy to be listened to without any interruption. On the way home, his wife remarked, 'Everyone was so pleased with you.'

He asked, 'Were they?'

'Indeed,' said his wife. 'One colleague said you were dynamic, one said you were so interesting, and another said you were remarkable.'

That's the power of listening.

About Being an Influential Listener:

Listening is the most effective and yet the most neglected part of communication. When you listen, you gain knowledge that you would never have gained any other way. We all love to talk. And when we listen, we do it with the intention of interrupting and responding.

When you train yourself to become an active listener, you may hear nonsense, weird ideas, bizarre opinions and bad comments. But that's a small price to pay for the lifetime of learning that you will gain through listening.

Stephen Covey in his magnum opus *The 7 Habits of Highly Effective People* writes, 'Seek first to understand, then to be understood.' He highlights listening as one of the key habits. Listening makes the other person feel important. By knowing what others are thinking, how they are feeling, what their viewpoints are, we will be able to transform situations, formulate ideas and forge better connections.

Without being involved, no one can be an influential listener. Influential listening means giving one's undivided attention to the speaker, not turning the spotlight on yourself however tempted you are to do that, not attempting to fix problems or provide solutions, but encouraging them.

Everyone wants to feel cared. Listening demonstrates care. So, listen. And see the difference it makes to your life and career.

Action Points

Cultivate deep and active listening:

1. Always look directly at the speaker.
2. Avoid getting distracted with your own thoughts or the goings-on around you.
3. Indicate with your actions that you are listening.

Respond thoughtfully:

1. Do not form any judgements.
2. Provide feedback that is specific, actionable and focused on the content of the message.
3. Connect with the speaker's message.

Foster a safe and encouraging environment:

1. Do not interrupt.
2. Acknowledge the speaker's emotions and perspectives, even if you disagree with them.
3. Show appreciation for the speaker's willingness to share their thoughts and experiences.

Remember,

Listening is not only hearing others with an active intention, but as author Tanveer Naseer says, giving them space to contribute.

17

Help Others

People really need help but may attack you
if you do help them. Help people anyway.
— Dr Kent M. Keith

Argentinian golfer Roberto de Vincenzo won the PGA Tour Championship and with it, a large sum of prize money. At the end of the day, he left the club, and as he was starting his car, a poor woman approached him. With tears in her eyes, she said, 'My child will die if surgery is not performed urgently, and I don't have the money for the operation.'

Without thinking for a moment, he took out his pen and signed the cheque over to the woman. The following week, when he appeared at the club, a golfing official met him and said, 'You gave away the winner's cheque to a woman who conned you. There is no sick child. She fleeced you.'

'You mean there is no baby who is dying?' asked the legendary golfer.

'That's right,' said the official.

Heaving a sigh of relief, Roberto said, 'That's the best news I've heard all week.'

This is an unbelievable tale. Roberto not only helps without thinking twice, but he doesn't expect anything in return either. On the contrary, when he is told that he has been cheated, he is happy to know that there is no dying child.

About Helping Others:

We all need help. Even if you don't get help when you need it, do not deny others the help that you can give. Often, we are not aware of what we are good at and we spend time doing things for which we have average or below average competency. But if someone could help us identify those strengths and guide us to make effective use of them, what a transformation it would bring! We would be immensely grateful to that person, wouldn't we? Be that person.

Help people discover their talents, skills and gifts, tell them how they can make better use of their strengths. If you are a manager, give them opportunities within or outside the department where they can make better use of their strengths. Train, coach, mentor, listen, ask, support; there are many ways in which you can lend a helping hand.

Look around you, you will see a co-worker struggling with his project, or another co-worker who is stressed because she can't get a proposal right or someone who is trying to solve a problem but is not able to find a solution. Please help them.

Facilitating the development of others will earn you their respect and add to your influence. You lose nothing by helping others because helping others is an investment in yourself. By extending a hand, you cultivate a rich network, acquire new skills and gain invaluable perspectives.

Action Points

Cultivate a helping mindset:

1. Understand the challenges and perspectives of others.
2. Volunteer your time.
3. Advocate for your colleagues by supporting their career development.

Build supportive relationships and encourage others:

1. Listen to the concerns of others (that's one of the best ways to help a colleague or anyone else).
2. Ask if you can help a struggling colleague in any way.
3. Offer words of encouragement.

Act based on your strengths and resources:

1. Share your knowledge and learning.
2. Provide constructive feedback.
3. Contribute your skills to achieve shared goals.

Remember,

Your success is often measured by the success of others.

18

Abandon Why, Adopt How

To ask the right question is already half the solution of a problem.
—Carl Jung

Zoe and Mac were colleagues. Both were expecting to be promoted. But both their bosses informed them that they were not being considered for the promotion.

Eventually, both went to see their managers. They wanted to know why they were being overlooked for the promotion.

The response from their managers was. 'You are not ready to step up yet.'

But Zoe and Mac handled the question differently. While Zoe asked *why*, Mac asked *how*.

Zoe said, 'Why do you think I am not ready yet?'

By asking why, Zoe gave a tailor-made situation to her boss to list down all her shortcomings. And the boss did exactly that. The boss highlighted where she was lacking and where she was not up to the mark. As a result, Zoe came back angry and upset.

On the other hand, Mac asked his boss, 'How can I prove to you that I am ready to step up?'

This response forced his boss to elaborate on what evidence Mac needed to provide.

Both faced the same situation. But while Zoe ended up without finding a solution to the problem, because she asked the wrong question, Mac emerged successful because he asked the right one.

About Abandoning Why, Adopting How:

Asking *Why* is taking a step backward. Asking *How* is moving a step forward. What had to happen has already happened. There's no point in asking *Why* now? Yes, do the root cause analysis and whatever you need to do as a process formality or compliance requirement. But there's not much you can do by going on asking: 'Why, why, why?' Because you will just be stuck with the problem.

When you focus on *How*, your mind starts looking for solutions. Why isn't something working? versus how can we make this work? See the difference between the two. Asking the *why* questions will trigger negativity and a defensive approach. Lots of explanations and rationalizations will happen. But the *how* questions will spark curiosity and inspire creativity.

When you use this approach at work, you will emerge as a go-to-person because you would have built a reputation of someone who believes in action, forward-thinking and solution seeking. So, open the door to possibilities by abandoning the *Why* and adopting the *How*.

When you ask *Why*, it makes the respondent defensive. They start believing that they are being accused of something. They simply retreat into a shell. *Why* questions should be restricted only for situations and cases, not for dealing with people.

Action Points

Embrace experimentation and learning:

1. Be open-minded enough to ask open-ended questions.
2. Asking the right questions is important, but asking the right person is more important.
3. Invite discussions with your questions.

Develop a solution oriented mindset:

1. Identify the desired outcome.
2. Focus on actionable steps.
3. Find new ways to tackle situations.

Don't let a problem become an excuse:

1. Positive possibilities abound in a problem. Look for them.
2. Don't react negatively to a problem. Respond positively.
3. Choose how you want the problem to affect you.

Remember,

The question 'why' is often exploratory, aiming to understand the underlying factors, whereas 'how' is solution-oriented, seeking practical steps.

19

Be Creative

*Creativity is seeing what others see and thinking
what no one else ever thought.*

—Albert Einstein

At 3M, every employee has an hour a day to do whatever they want. It could be anything. From working on a side project to pursuing their hobby.

That one hour is entirely theirs. What they do in that hour may or may not be directly relevant to their work. They don't have to justify it to their boss either. Whatever they come up with, they are supposed to share with their colleagues. That's the only requirement.

This is a brilliant way to foster creativity. 3M is giving the message that 'We have hired you; we think you are smart and we trust you to find solutions.'

About Being Creative:

Ideas, ideas, ideas. One idea can change the fortune of your company. One idea can make you a champion at the workplace. Being creative is the way to stardom at work.

Do not work blindly. Observe what's happening in your department and in the company. Seek opportunities. Nothing is perfect. There's always room for improvement. Don't wait to do something enormous. Little things mean a lot. A series of quick wins can lead to big results.

Start your creative process by eliminating the unnecessary. Don't be afraid to ask silly questions. Do not worry about other people's reactions. Those who are unprofessional will laugh. The professionals will understand. Challenging the status quo requires courage and confidence. And of course, creativity.

If you wait for inspiration to get creative, then you may have to wait forever. So, do your bit every day. So many activities, processes, transactions must be happening daily in your organization, look at them one by one. Analyse them from the viewpoint of cost, speed, efficiency and quality. Invent and experiment.

Once you establish your reputation as a creative person, there'll be no end to your progress. Creativity and innovation, according to media executive Bob Iger, is the heart and soul of the company. So what are you waiting for . . . become your company's heart and soul by being creative.

Creativity is the top skill that attracts recruiters because it helps in building better teamwork and increases problem solving.

Action Points

Explore:

1. Challenge conformity.

2. Challenge yourself and the team by implementing certain restrictions (like not using certain words or tools).
3. Collaborate with colleagues from diverse departments.

Take a different approach:

1. Be with people who think differently.
2. Seek inspiration from different sources.
3. Become an active observer.

Be ready to embrace new ideas:

1. Present unconventional solutions.
2. Take calculated risks.
3. Maintain a creative workspace (maybe have a brainstorming wall).

Remember,

Creativity is a universal trait, not an exclusive privilege. Imagination, curiosity and a willingness to challenge the norm are the building blocks accessible to all.

20

Keep Your Word

*I would rather be accused of breaking precedents
than breaking promises.*

—John Kennedy

Abraham Lincoln was famous for his honesty and integrity. Here's a story about how he kept his word, even after years had passed.

Once Lincoln was travelling with a military man, a colonel from the state of Kentucky, who offered him a drink. Lincoln politely refused. Some time later, his companion reached into his pocket and brought out some cigars. He said, 'You didn't drink with me, but I hope you will take a smoke with me.'

Lincoln said, 'You are such a fine gentleman to travel with, maybe I ought to take a smoke with you. But before I do so, let me share a story with you, an experience I had when I was a small boy.'

And he narrated the following story:

'One day when I was about nine years or so, my mother called me and said, "My son, the doctor tells me I won't get well. But before I go, I want you to promise me that you will never drink and smoke as long as you live." I gave my mother my word.

And up to this hour, Colonel, I have kept my promise. Now, would you suggest that I break my word and take a smoke with you?'

The Colonel replied, 'Certainly not, Mr Lincoln. I wouldn't have you do it for the world.'

Lincoln had made the promise ages ago, but he had not broken it. That's the value your word should have. Not for nothing was he called *Honest Abe*.

About Keeping Your Word:

The foundation of trust and respect is the habit of keeping your word. Breaking promises shatters the trust and respect that people may have in you. And once there's a crack in your reputation, it is impossible to regain that trust and respect, no matter what you do. So, be very careful with your commitments.

Don't play with your honour. Your word is as good as your honour. So, if you say you will do something, you had better do it. If you promise to finish a task by an agreed deadline, you ought to keep that promise. Yes, on many occasions, due to dependency on other stakeholders, you may not be able to meet the promised deadline. In such cases, you need to inform the project owner/s about the impending delay.

Keeping promises establishes a connection with people because it is the essence of integrity. The value of your personal brand rises. People look up to you. In any organization, reliability and dependability play an important role. When your co-workers and clients know that you can be relied and depended upon, it means that you have established trust in your company. Not keeping your word can harm your name permanently and prove costly to the company by way of missed opportunities and damaged relationships.

Be known as a person of integrity. This will give people around you a feeling of security. Who doesn't want to feel secure? Honouring your word plays a powerful role in how you are viewed by your co-workers. Making a promise means a moral obligation. So, do not take it lightly.

Action Points

Be mindful:

1. Do not over-promise.
2. Commit only what you know or think you can do.
3. Don't be in a hurry to give your word.

Demonstrate reliability and accountability:

1. Once you make a promise, fulfil it.
2. Deliver on your commitments.
3. Take ownership if, due to extraordinary circumstances, you fail to meet a deadline.

Communicate effectively:

1. Highlight challenges that might hinder your ability to meet the commitment.
2. Offer alternative solutions should your initial commitment meet with obstacles.
3. Keep all stakeholders updated.

Remember,

You become worthy by keeping your word
and worthless by breaking your word.

21

Never Stop Learning

Learning is not attained by chance, it must be sought
for with ardor and attended to with diligence.

—Abigail Adams

Stuart is an entrepreneur who owns a successful business. Before starting his own business, he worked in numerous sectors in different managerial roles. He knows international shipping, how to identify multi-bagger stocks, and the ins and outs of owning a successful art gallery. He has a varied experience and has nothing left to prove to himself or to others. So, he could be excused, if he were content to ride out the status quo.

But Stuart is not one to rest on his laurels because he has a never-stop-learning mentality. He had already achieved much in the first half of his career and, to make a mark in the second half, he knew that his skills needed to evolve. Digitization is in, so he registered himself as a student of the Digital Marketing Science course to hone his digital marketing skills.

'I always challenge myself,' he says. 'I have to keep learning all the time.'

When I asked him if he didn't feel odd being the oldest student in the class, he said, 'I always want to be relevant.'

That's the spirit we should all have. The never-stop-learning attitude is the only way to be relevant in this fast-changing world.

About Never Stop Learning:

Everyone is a teacher. But alas, there aren't that many students. We are all eager to teach but only a handful want to learn. If you want to lead, you must learn, because all leaders are learners. If we are willing to learn, then we can learn from every interaction we have, every individual we meet, every situation we encounter, every book that we read, every moment that we live.

You may think some people are better or smarter than you. They are the learners who have applied their learnings in their work area. They have capitalized on the knowledge and information they have gained. You can also do the same. I am not telling you to compete with them. I am stressing the point that you must compete with yourself. Get better every day.

Brian Tracy in his book *Victory!* lists down seven questions you can ask yourself to know what learning you need at the workplace. I am mentioning three of them below:

- What do you do easily and well that seems to be difficult for others?
- Of all the things you do, what contributes the greatest value to your work and your company?
- What part of your work most interests and fascinates you?

Likewise, you can ask many more. Once you are aware of where you need to focus, you can learn the right stuff that can make a difference to you and your career. You will become more relevant; you will develop new perspectives and your competencies will increase, giving a boost to your confidence.

To unleash your full potential, never stop learning.

Action Points

Integrate learning into your daily routine:

1. Dedicate time for focused learning. Set aside an hour or whatever time you can spare to read, listen to podcasts and take online courses.
2. Get a mentor or a professional coach.
3. Apply what you learn at the workplace.

Embrace curiosity:

1. Actively seek knowledge by asking questions and exploring new topics.
2. Transform everyday situations into lessons.
3. Challenge yourself with new things.

Cultivate a learning community and utilize resources:

1. Be around people who have a passion for learning.
2. Take advantage of free online learning resources.
3. Make your learning enjoyable by choosing learning activities that are interesting.

Remember,

The day you stop learning, you start stagnating, which means you stop living, which means you start dying.

22

Be a Crisis Manager

The secret of crisis management is not good vs bad, it's
preventing the bad from getting worse.
—Andy Gilman

In February 2018, KFC faced a unique situation: the shortage
of chicken. Imagine the severity of the crisis. KFC's business
depends on chicken, and they did not have enough. They had to
shut down more than half of their 900 stores in the UK.

The shortage was a result of delivery failure. KFC
had switched its contract to a new delivery partner, DHL,
which had to cancel or delay several deliveries because of
'administrative issues'.

KFC's predicament became big news. Social and
mainstream media had a field day. Customers vented on Twitter.
The pressure was enormous. But it is during such times that the
resilience of an organization is known.

KFC's management rose to the task. Even as they
struggled to get restaurants to reopen, they ran a high profile,
humorous apology.

The bright red advertisement showed an empty bucket with the chain's initials scrambled to say 'FCK' on it. Below it, the caption read,

A chicken restaurant without any chicken. It's not ideal. Huge apologies to our customers, especially those who traveled out of their way to find we were closed.

The deft handling of the crisis drew appreciation from one and all and KFC became the poster child on how to tactfully handle a crisis.

About Being a Crisis Manager:

Crises are inevitable.

At some point in time in your career, you are going to face one. You might crack or become stronger. It all depends on how you handle it.

Generally, people baulk when a crisis occurs. They either panic or freeze. Train yourself mentally to manage a crisis when it happens. Spend some time rehearsing in your mind the actions you will take, the instructions that you will give and the ways you will keep yourself from succumbing to pressure.

You might think *crises will differ in their severity*. That's true. Crises may certainly differ, but the techniques to manage them are not going to change. Calmness, coolness and control, these are the three traits one must demonstrate in a crisis. So work on those traits.

If a crisis cannot be avoided, at least it shouldn't be allowed to worsen. True leadership is revealed in the crucible of crisis. When you take the lead in managing it, you show that you have leadership skills and have grit, guts and gumption.

Anticipate crises well in advance. If you know what works for you, you should also know what to do if it stops working.

Think of alternate scenarios. If things go wrong suddenly, you should know what to do to set them right.

Action Points

Cultivate essential skills and knowledge:

1. Understand what crises your company could face.
2. Train yourself to respond with speed, rather than precision.
3. Sharpen your decision-making abilities.

Be prepared always:

1. Develop a crisis management plan to handle various scenarios.
2. Identify potential threats and vulnerabilities.
3. Stay up to date on crisis management strategies and best practices.

Enhance your emotional intelligence:

1. Practice calmness.
2. Eliminate knee-jerk reactions; focus on appropriate responses.
3. Remain engaged always.

Remember,

A crisis doesn't mean the end of the world.
It means the beginning of new learning.

23

Have a Growth Mindset

If you can get 1 percent better each day for one year,
you'll end up thirty-seven times better by the time you're done.

—James Clear

Who doesn't know the story of the hare and the tortoise? The average speed of a tortoise is roughly 0.12 to 0.25 mph. The Guinness Book of World Records registers the speed of the fastest tortoise as 0.63 mph. In contrast, the hare runs at a speed of 50 mph. The difference in their speed is mind-boggling. Yet, the tortoise won the race against the hare.

How was this possible?

The race between the hare and the tortoise was not a matter of speed. It was a battle between a Fixed Mindset and Growth Mindset.

The tortoise did not believe that it was slow. It boldly decided to contest despite knowing the superiority of its rival. The tortoise demonstrated a growth mindset.

The hare, on the other hand, was arrogant about its speed. It lost because it approached the race with the fixed mindset of 'I am fast, therefore I will win even if I take a nap.'

This tale shows how a growth mindset can bring remarkable results.

About Having a Growth Mindset:

Cultivate a growth mindset. A fixed mindset limits you, makes you believe that you are incapable of doing certain tasks because you possess a certain set of traits like skill or intelligence that is unlikely to change. On the other hand, a growth mindset doesn't limit you because of your inherent characteristics, but makes you believe that you can learn and grow.

A growth mindset is the most important ingredient for success. Carol Dweck, a psychologist, professor and researcher, in her book *Mindset: The New Psychology of Success* states that 'Becoming is better than being.' No one is born extraordinary. They become extraordinary. Ability alone will not help you. Ability is like a flash in the pan. Vinod Kambli was a gifted batsman and was a delight to watch. He was endowed with exceptional abilities yet he failed to achieve the kind of success he could have. Ability, combined with effort, can throw open the door to unimaginable possibilities for you.

Dweck makes another vital point. In the fixed mindset, everything is about the outcome. The growth mindset allows people to value what they are doing regardless of the outcome. With a growth mindset, you can freely embrace challenges, build resilience, develop your intelligence and abilities and accept failures as learning opportunities.

A growth mindset is never restrictive. It helps you do things that you are not confident about. Whether you are good at them or not doesn't matter. You just take the leap. Dweck asks a very poignant question. 'If you are somebody when you are successful, what are you when you are unsuccessful?' The answer is simple. A fixed mindset makes you think that way. You must prove yourself, again and again. But in a growth mindset, setbacks are learning curves.

Action Points

View setbacks as stepping stones:

1. Stop perceiving difficulties as failures.
2. Consider problems as challenges.
3. Consider challenges as opportunities.

Change your approach:

1. Replace the word 'failing' with 'learning'.
2. Use the word 'yet' (instead of saying I can't, say I can't yet).
3. Identify negative self-talk that might be hindering your progress.

Visualize:

1. Mentally see yourself achieving your goals.
2. See yourself doing tasks that you have never done before.
3. Use sketches and diagrams to visually organize your thoughts and information.

Remember,

A growth mindset fuels a relentless pursuit of progress.
It's the belief that abilities can be developed
through dedication and hard work.

24

Stand Out by Being Memorable

The world accommodates you for fitting in,
but only rewards you for standing out.
—Matshona Dhliwayo

Ali Raza always stood out from the crowd. He was not exceptionally brilliant or a subject matter expert.

But what he could do was create memorable moments. Whether in dealing with his manager or with his team members or any other co-worker, he had his own special way of making things interesting, comfortable and pleasing.

He was always *first with a purpose.* While others took care of their stuff, he would do something visibly worthwhile for the company. Like working on a project that others were reluctant to work on. He made a reputation for himself by doing *something specific*, like supporting struggling colleagues. He never talked about problems but whenever he heard of problems, he would immediately *start thinking of solutions*, irrespective of whose project it was.

To stand out, you must be different.

About Standing Out:

Be a master at something. Have one skill that defines you. Be consistently reliable. Going the extra mile is not enough. See what lies ahead of that extra mile. And then take a few more steps. Whenever you have a choice to make between two paths—like Robert Frost—take the path that is less trodden. That will make the difference. Create magical moments when the going gets tough.

You might not be an expert but if you can get things done by taking responsibility and working through obstacles, you can really make the experience memorable. This way, you become super valuable to the team and the organization. Don't just build a track record of doing right things the right way in the right time. When the smooth sea turns turbulent, know how to calm the turbulence.

You can stand out by ensuring that the bad doesn't turn worse and making the already good better. No one will tell you to do this. You must seize the opportunity, take the initiative and understand what's happening around you. There is always room for improvement. There is always a chance to shine. Of course, when you shine, you will invite resentment. But don't let that trouble you. Continue being respectful and empathetic.

When you make people feel worthy and significant, you become memorable for them. You will experience greater fulfilment and a sense of accomplishment. Doing small, ordinary things exceptionally well will make you an outstanding resource.

Action Points

Develop a unique personality:

1. Highlight your strengths and passions.
2. Think innovatively.
3. Be a storyteller.

Make meaningful connections:

1. Listen as if the speaker is the most important person for you.
2. Go the extra mile for someone.
3. Celebrate the success of others.

Create positive impressions:

1. End interactions on a cheerful note.
2. Always be encouraging.
3. Refine your communication style.

Remember,

> By following, you can only fit in.

25

Experiment

The true method of knowledge is experiment.
—William Blake

If you haven't heard of *The 5 Monkeys Experiment*, let me share it with you. Although there is controversy around whether it happened, there are lessons to be learnt even if we consider it as an analogy.

The experiment goes like this:

Five monkeys are in a cage. Outside the cage is a bunch of bananas. When monkey number One goes for the bananas, the researcher throws buckets of cold water on all five monkeys.

Sometime later, monkey number Two goes for the bananas. The researcher once again throws buckets of cold water on all five monkeys. The researcher then keeps the buckets away and doesn't touch them again.

Now, when monkey number Three tries to go for the bananas, the other four monkeys attack him and restrain him from touching the bananas. They are afraid of the punishment.

Some moments later, the researcher replaces monkey number One with a new monkey, who wasn't part of the experiment and thus has never had cold water thrown on him. As soon as the new monkey reaches for the bananas, the other four monkeys pounce on him, stopping him from doing so. When he tries again, the other four monkeys subdue him once more. The new monkey understands that if he goes for the bananas, he will be attacked. So, he stops.

The researcher replaces monkey number Two with another new monkey. When this monkey is tempted by the bananas, the other four monkeys attack him, including the new monkey who never had cold water thrown on him.

The researcher continues to replace all the monkeys, one at a time, until all five original monkeys are out. Each time the new monkey tries to grab the bananas, the others attack him, even though these monkeys had never been punished by the researcher when they had tried to reach for the bananas.

Thus, the new monkeys, who have never faced the punishment of cold water, learn that they shouldn't go for the bananas.

The conclusion drawn from this experiment is that the monkeys stopped going for the bananas because *that's the way it's always been done*.

Aren't most of us like this? We don't experiment because we are suffering from the 5 Monkey Experiment syndrome.

About Experimenting:

Imagine if Thomas Alva Edison had given up after a series of failed experiments. God only knows how much time it would have taken the world to invent the electric bulb. Progress means experimenting.

Start small. Do some itsy-bitsy changes in the way you work. Experiment on yourself. See how it affects you and your work. If there's a negative or no impact, then stick to the way you were doing it. No outcome or a negative outcome doesn't mean you stop experimenting. Experiment on your other work habits and styles. You are bound to see some positive impact here and there; that should give you the impetus to aim for some quick wins in your work area.

Go through the processes, make a workflow diagram, strike out a step and see if the flow remains the same or gets affected or improves. First focus on the simplest process. Eliminate the steps that you think are not contributing to improvement. Once it works fine, share your experience with other stakeholders and get the changes done officially. As you gain confidence with your experimentation, shift your attention to more complex processes. Identify one of them and follow the same principles you did when you were experimenting with the simplest process. Celebrate the success. Learn from failure.

You can then look for improvements beyond your work area. Observe how processes happen in different departments. Share your inputs with the respective heads. If they agree with your suggestions, collaborate with them to get the changes done.

Experimenting constantly can give you joy, do away with work ennui and bring about a sense of accomplishment for you. Experiments fuel creativity and change and both are necessary for the organization's progress.

Action Points

Encourage innovation:

1. Be more curious and encourage curiosity.
2. What do you think? What else? Ask these questions to your team members.
3. Think of multiple solutions for every problem.

Experiment with daily tasks:

1. Don't just do your daily work blindly.
2. Alter your workflow slightly.
3. Explore different ways to communicate, instead of sending lengthy emails.

Take baby steps:

1. Begin with small-scale experiments.
2. Discuss beforehand your experiment ideas with your colleagues/seniors.
3. Document the process.

Remember,

Experimentation is the cornerstone of discovery.

26

Discover

The only way of discovering the limits of the possible is to
venture a little way past them into the impossible.
—Arthur C. Clarke

Nikhil was a sales maestro, conducting symphonies of solutions orchestrated around a single note: the customer.

He focused on what people cared about and what motivated them. He ensured that he and his sales team understood the customer's needs in the first meeting itself, so that they never had to repeat themselves.

Discovery was his instrument, and active listening, his virtuoso performance. He delved beyond the surface, seeking the heart of the customer's desires. The 'why' was his lodestar, illuminating a path to unparalleled understanding.

By placing the customer at the epicenter, Nikhil not only forged stronger bonds but also elevated the entire organization. His legacy is a testament to the power of empathy and insight in an era dominated by transactional relationships.

His 'discovery' approach—a blueprint for success—is applicable to any realm where human connection is paramount.

About Discovering:

The habit of discovering issues, problems, loopholes and deficiencies and knowing how to fix them can take you places. You can do anything in life.

Don't see things from a critical angle. Look at them from the improvement perspective. Don't scoff at what and how something is being done. Your predecessors did what was best then. Now, maybe, those best things seem ordinary. Make them extraordinary. Discover how you can do it.

You may also discover, as you go deep into policies, procedures and processes, that some things are being done incorrectly. Since it's a practice, no one ever bothered to even consider doing it in some other way. No one wanted to find out. No one was ready to discover. As Dave Stutman said, 'Complacency is the enemy of progress.'

Therefore, don't rest on your laurels. Go on exploring. Exploring will lead you to discovery. And discoveries lift our spirits, make the future more hopeful, paying off in a big way. When you set off on a discovery spree, it opens the floodgates to innovation. And innovation fosters a culture of continuous improvement.

So, wherever you are working. Or, for that matter, for everyday living also, if you wish to SHINE, then develop discovery tendencies. Find out what's wrong, what's ordinary and make them right and extraordinary.

Even when you are ahead of your game or think you are, remember, you will discover you still have a lot to learn.

Action Points

Utilize data and analytics:

1. Be data-driven because data-driven discovery can lead to more informed decision-making.
2. Leverage data analysis tools to identify trends, patterns and potential areas for improvement.
3. Keep questioning every solution that lacks data.

Be innovative:

1. Role play. Wear a customer's hat and from their perspective, try to prove a team member wrong about the company's product or service.
2. Form cross-functional teams to work on projects.
3. Recognize and reward discovery.

Try different strategies:

1. Don't accept the company's ready-made answers to problems. Find your own solutions.
2. Share learning from previous failures.
3. Tell juniors to question your ideas.

Remember,

Discovery is about seeing things with new eyes.

27

Think Simply

It is always the simple that produces the marvelous.

—Amelia Barr

This story is the stuff of legends.

In the 1950s, a well-known toothpaste company was going through tough times. It announced a company-wide competition to invite ideas that could boost sales. Several days passed, but no one could come up with an idea that could increase sales.

One day, an outsider approached the company and said that he had an innovative idea that would ensure an immediate 40 per cent increase in sales, without costing much for implementation. But he asked for $100,000 to share the idea. In the 1950s, that was a lot of money. Even today, $100,000 is a big amount.

The management's concern though was not the money because they knew that they could recover that amount in no time, considering the high volume of toothpaste sales. They were not sure if they should accept an idea from an outsider. After many weeks, when the company's employees were not able to come up with even one idea, the management team called the outsider and told him that they were ready to do the deal with him.

After the legal process was completed and the money was received by the outsider, he handed over a small slip of paper on which were written just four words. Isn't that unbelievable? Companies spend millions on innovation and the hired consulting companies then provide a comprehensive report that sometimes goes into hundreds of pages. But here was a gentleman, who in exchange for $100,000, had given just four words.

What were those words?

'Make the hole bigger.'

Earlier, the toothpaste tubes had an opening of about 5 mm for squeezing out the paste. By increasing the diameter of the hole from 5 mm to 6 mm, the volume of toothpaste squeezed out would increase by a whopping 40 per cent. So, the consumers would use more toothpaste and finish the tube faster and hence the need to buy more would arise, leading to a huge increase in sales.

This simple thinking created history for the company. So, 'think simply' even when the problem is complex.

About Thinking Simply:

Kazuo Inamori in his book, *A Compass to Fulfillment*, writes, 'The more complex a problem appears to be, the more we need to address it with decisions and actions based on simple principles.' Simple is considered, well, simple. Not much value is attached to it. The world loves complexity. To solve a simple issue, many complex actions will be taken. But the fact is, and as Kazuo Inamori advocates, complex issues can be solved by taking simple steps.

But taking those simple steps is extraordinarily difficult. Train yourself to think simply. When a problem arises or a crisis occurs, we immediately start focusing on the outcomes, when we shouldn't be doing that. We should instead concentrate on the process. Break the problem into chunks and address them one by one. Just as, hypothetically speaking, if you had to eat an elephant, you couldn't eat it at one go. But in bits and pieces, you would be able to consume the entire animal.

Complexity makes the problem more complex. And that's a sure way to disaster. To change anything, we must first change our thinking. Think simple ideas. Don't start thinking about changing the world. That's too far-fetched. Think simple ideas, and when you implement them, one by one, you are already on the way to bringing about a massive change.

Often, what appears complex is simple. Heisuke Hironaka, the world-famous mathematician, says, 'A complex phenomenon is merely the projection of a simple fact.' One just needs to change one's perspective of looking at the problem and things will become crystal clear.

Simplicity provides more clarity and focus. It is the shortest path to a solution. But simplicity is not simple. It is difficult, but by focusing on things that are important and disregarding things that are less important, you can master simplicity.

So put on your thinking hat. The one that will help you to THINK SIMPLY.

Action Points

Focus on the core issue:

1. Be attentive to the process.
2. Ask yourself these two questions: What are we trying to achieve? and What is the root cause of the issue?
3. Minimize complexity. Know that the problem may be complex but its solution need not be.

Clarity and conciseness are the key:

1. Prioritize ruthlessly; not all aspects of a problem hold equal importance.
2. Favour short and to the point communication. Don't bury your points under layers of information.
3. Eliminate unnecessary tasks.

Practise mindfulness techniques:

1. Meditate.
2. Protect your mental space.
3. Focus on the present moment.

Remember,

The more complex the problem,
the more you need to think simply.

28

Visualize

*Visualize this thing that you want, see it, feel it,
believe in it. Make your mental blueprint, and begin.*
—Robert Collier

Darren Hardy, author of *The Compound Effect*, is a firm believer
of visualization techniques.

He found his dream wife by practicing one of those
techniques.

Hardy would go to bars and attend events, thinking that
he would find her at some place or the other, but after some
time, he realized that he was not doing the right thing. So he
implemented the method of visualization.

He wrote down exactly what he was looking for in a
woman. Every single detail. He ended up writing about forty
pages in which he had vividly described what his future wife
should look like. But that wasn't enough!

He realized that to marry such a woman, he needed to be
a different man, someone who truly deserved such a prize. So,
he wrote another forty pages about what kind of a man he had

to become. He was specific about what he wanted and thus was able to visualize clearly.

Visualization is a powerful tool to achieve your goals and realize your dreams.

About Visualizing:

You have an audacious goal. Or an outrageous dream. Something so staggering in enormity that you don't want to even think of it, and so you push it to the back of your mind. Don't do that. Never think that the targets that are set in your organization are unattainable. Use the power of visualization to achieve that audacious goal, that outrageous dream.

Every day, set aside a few moments from your life to visualize. Visualization should always be about what you want, not about what you don't want. Most of us keep visualizing the dreadful things that may happen to us. We will be laid off, we will get a poor appraisal, we will fail, we will make a mistake, we can't do this, and so on and so forth. If, instead, we spent that time visualizing about things that we wanted, imagine what we could achieve.

Don't we all agree that seeing is believing? We should apply the same logic to ourselves. Have a vivid picture of what you want in your mind, what you want to achieve, and keep seeing that picture daily for as long as it takes you to believe it and transform it into reality. By practising visualization, you will be able to shift your mind in the right direction. Many famous people have used the power of visualization with great success. Richard Bach, author of *Jonathan Livingston Seagull*, has publicly stated that he was able to finish his book because of creative visualization.

Nothing has ever been achieved unless it was first conceived in the mind. If you can conceive it in your mind, you can achieve it.

Programme yourself in such a way that you start living, breathing, eating, sleeping that audacious goal and outrageous dream, until your vision becomes your version of reality.

Action Points

Become a visual thinker:

1. Imagine your future as the present.
2. Incorporate visualizations regularly into your meetings and presentations.
3. Use visual aids like whiteboards, mind maps, online collaborative tools.

Choose the right technique for the task:

1. Experiment with different approaches like mental imagery, sketching and digital tools to discover what works best for you in different situations.
2. Look at examples of effective visualizations online or in design magazines.
3. Do the Balance Wheel exercise—it focuses on identifying and evaluating different areas of your life to achieve better balance which can indirectly set the stage for improved visualization.

Lead by example:

1. Write in detail what you want to do.
2. Take actions that take you towards your goal and run that vision in your mind.
3. Encourage others to think visually.

Remember,

Your mind is the architect of your reality.
Visualize your masterpiece.

29

Appreciate

I've learned that people will forget what you said,
people will forget what you did, but people
will never forget how you made them feel.

—Dr Maya Angelou

Alex Jacob—a rising star in the company—was known for his sharp intellect and unwavering dedication. Yet, despite his achievements, there was a growing sense of dissatisfaction. His work, while demanding, had become monotonous. The once-thrilling challenges were now routine tasks.

One day, while engrossed in a particularly mundane project, he overheard a conversation between his deputy, Sweety Singh, and a new employee. Sweety was offering genuine praise for the newcomer's small accomplishment, highlighting its importance to the team. Alex was struck by the sincerity in her voice. It was in stark contrast to how he and other managers managed and were managed. They neither appreciated nor were they appreciated.

Inspired by Sweety, Alex decided to shift his perspective. He began to actively appreciate the work of his colleagues. A simple 'thank you' for a completed task, a genuine compliment on a well-executed project, or even a supportive word during a challenging time became his new norm.

The transformation was gradual but profound. His team's morale soared. People felt valued, motivated and more invested in their work. Productivity increased, and the once mundane tasks began to take on new meaning. Alex realized that while individual contributions were essential, it was the collective spirit, fostered by mutual appreciation, that truly drove success.

The experience taught him that the most significant rewards often come not from personal accolades, but from the impact one can make on the lives of others. And in the realm of business, as in life, appreciation is the most valuable currency of all.

About Appreciating:

If you want to see an instant miracle, praise someone. The moment you say appreciative words to another person, their whole being blossoms. So much positivity runs through them that you can feel that positive energy. At the workplace, the best way to lift the morale of a team member or the team is to appreciate their contribution.

According to human resource consulting firm, Robert Half, appreciation is one of the three factors that make employees happy. Yet we tend to neglect appreciating our co-workers. Whether others are appreciative about you or not, you should not hesitate to appreciate your team members, peers and even your seniors. Be quick to compliment, show large-heartedness by using glowing (but genuine) terms to recognize their effort, contribution and work. Sometimes even a simple 'Thank you' can work wonders.

Appreciation is a powerful tool for everybody to use at the workplace. It's not just for managers and seniors. Also, remember that appreciation is not only reserved for star employees. The unsung heroes, those working without displaying any flair and style, should also be praised.

You will find ample opportunities to appreciate others. Compliment co-workers for a job well done, for specific skills that they have, for their enthusiasm and positivity, for their exemplary teamwork, for their attitude, for their commitment . . . the reasons are endless.

If everyone in the organization were to be appreciative of others, engagement scores would shoot up and a solid culture of gratitude would be established.

Action Points

Express gratitude regularly:

1. Recognize potential and acknowledge publicly.
2. Thank colleagues individually.
3. Highlight the specific action or behaviour while expressing appreciation.

Celebrate:

1. Have team lunches and/or outings.
2. Give away prizes, trophies and awards.
3. Implement peer-to-peer recognition programmes.

Promote open communication:

1. Give constructive feedback.
2. Give your time.
3. If mistakes happen, focus on solutions, not finding fault.

Remember,

> A single word of appreciation can be a
> lifeline to someone's spirit.

30

Know the Difference Between
Kindness and Niceness

*Niceness is all about what we do when other people are
looking. Kindness, on the other hand, runs deep.*
—Sangu Mandanna

Suresh Mohan did his work well, but when it came to promotions, he was overlooked by his manager. Once Suresh asked his manager why he wasn't getting promoted despite doing good work? His manager said, 'Because you are nice.'

Suresh was shocked by this response. He wondered how one could be denied a promotion for such a reason. He asked his manager for an explanation. His manager said, 'By being nice, you are protecting yourself from discomfort. You avoid having tough and hard conversations with your team members for fear of being considered not nice. That's not the way of professionals.'

'So, I should stop being kind?' Suresh asked.

'No, Suresh. You are getting confused. I never said you should not be kind.'

'But you just said that professionals should stop being nice.'

'Yes, absolutely,' his manager said. 'If you wish to grow, you should stop being nice because niceness is a self-motivated behaviour that is aimed at being liked and being seen in a positive light by others. Kindness, on the other hand, is motivated by caring for others.'

Suresh said, 'Sir, can you please elaborate on this?'

'Let me give you an example,' his manager said. 'Let's suppose that a team member of yours does not have the right attitude. As his supervisor, it is your duty and responsibility to highlight his shortcomings to him, yet you avoid doing it. You are being nice to him so that he doesn't dislike you and you seem nice to him. There's a selfish motive involved. But if you really felt for him, then you wouldn't stop yourself from giving him such vital feedback. You wouldn't care what he thought of you. Your intention would be to make him better because you truly cared for him. That's kindness. It is a selfless move.'

About Knowing the Difference between Kindness and Niceness:

Houston Kraft, author of *Deep Kindness*, says, 'Kindness is proactive and care-oriented, whereas niceness is more reactive and I-oriented. You can be kind but not nice and be nice but not kind.'

Being nice can stop you from being genuine. You may hesitate in pointing out a co-worker's mistake because you don't want him or her to feel bad, but in reality you don't want him or her to think bad about you. You are bothered about your reputation of being a nice person. You don't want it to shatter in your co-worker's eyes. So you keep quiet. You are being nice here but not genuine.

Often you hear people saying, 'He was just being nice.' What does this imply? That he was not sincere. Fear of rejection, fear of upsetting someone stops us from being our natural self. So being nice is being selfish. We are nice because we are expecting something in return. We are nice on condition that the outcome of our niceness should result in something positive for us.

Kindness has no such conditions. When we are kind, we are not bothered about the outcome. Positive or negative, it doesn't matter. We are not kind because we expect something in return. We are being kind because we are made that way. Kindness is inherent to us.

Let me highlight the difference with an example: A co-worker is underperforming. If you are nice, you will not disclose news about their underperformance because you don't want to get into a difficult conversation. But if you are kind, you will tell them and also help them to get better without expecting any credit or reward for helping.

If we are nice, we will have trouble putting across our point, correcting someone, standing up for what's right. If we are kind, we can freely express ourselves, be assertive and make positive changes because our communication would be straight and honest.

To make a difference at the workplace, know when to be nice and when to be kind. Kindness is a better goal as it indicates an ethical significance.

Action Points

Consider the motivation behind your action:

1. Ask yourself, *Why am I doing this?*
2. If your primary motivation is to help someone without expecting anything in return, you are being kind, but
3. If it is to gain favour or look good in someone's eyes, you are being nice.

Look at the impact of your action:

1. What's the potential outcome of your action? Does it empower or make someone feel good momentarily?
2. If it makes someone feel good fleetingly, you are being nice, but
3. If it creates a positive ripple effect, you are being kind.

Observe consistency:

1. Kindness is a consistent character trait, so if you are kind, you will be demonstrating care and compassion regularly. So, observe your actions closely.
2. Niceness is situational, so make sure you are not being pleasant in public, while being unpleasant in private.

Remember,

When you are nice, your intention is to please,
but when you are kind, your intention is to help.

31

Be Influential

You don't have to be a 'person of influence' to be influential.
—Scott Adams

Anyone else would have given up after being shot three times in the head, but not Malala.

She grew up in north-west Pakistan, where the Taliban had banned girls from attending school. Instead of being silenced by the attempt to kill her, she became a vocal supporter of female education.

She was an ordinary schoolgirl like millions of others but her determination to bring about change made her different from everyone else. In her own small way, she fought for the right to education.

One doesn't need a title or a position or power to influence. Every individual can do it. But one must decide to do it. Malala decided to do it.

'How dare the Taliban take away my basic right to education?' she asked in a speech when she was hardly eleven years old. This shows that age is no barrier to being influential.

By taking small, actionable steps that influence company processes, policies, procedures and people, you can introduce changes that can spark a revolution in your company and take it to greater heights.

About Being Influential:

You don't have to be a leader to be influential, though if you are influential, you can go on to become a leader. Influence is charisma and respect, rolled into one. Whether you are starting at your job or are the Chief Executive Officer, you can wield influence.

If you are influential at work, you are noticed, you get promotions faster, superiors talk about you, you establish connections with people inside and outside the organization, and you can make your team work well together.

Become trustworthy. That's the first step towards being influential. Be approachable. You can influence people only if they are comfortable with you. Be a patient listener. That's another key requirement. Display confidence, not arrogance. Give importance to people. Be up to date about what's going on in the organization. Believe in yourself and believe in your co-workers' skill and talent. Set an example. Have an open mind and impactful body language. Think big, for yourself and for others. Speak at every available opportunity. Be prepared. Stay connected with people around you and even with those who are far away.

In a paper published by McKinsey & Company titled *When Execution Isn't Enough: Decoding Inspirational Leadership* by Claudio Feser, nine influential tactics are described. They are:

Request, Legitimizing, Coalition, Rational persuasion, Socializing, Exchange, Personal appeal, Consultation, Inspirational appeals.

Use any or all these tactics to effectively influence team members, peers and other colleagues.

Action Points

Develop credibility and expertise:

1. Keep your skills and knowledge up to date.
2. Strive to become an expert in your field.
3. Consistently deliver high-quality work.

Build relationships:

1. Know your manager's goals.
2. Support your manager in problem-solving.
3. Share your knowledge.

Be passionate and persuasive in advocating ideas:

1. Present your ideas in ways that align with your company's goals.
2. Believe in the value of your ideas and convey that confidence and enthusiasm to others.
3. Be prepared to address the concerns of others with data, evidence and other alternative solutions.

Remember,

> Wherever you are and whatever you are,
> you can be influential.

32

Make Your Co-Workers Shine

As we work to create light for others,
we naturally light our own way.

— Mary Anne Radmacher

I had the privilege of working with a manager whose sole aim was to make his team shine. He never left his team in the dark. He would elaborately say what he expected from everyone; he made his priorities known to us.

Not only this, he helped us to prioritize our to-do lists, so that we could all be on the same page. He celebrated with us when we reached even the smallest milestone.

He never waited for us to go to him for support; he would offer help himself. He never interfered in the way we worked; rather, he empowered us to take our own decisions and never nagged us.

He inspired us with stories from his own life and from what he had read. He made himself available to us, by having 'open office' time reserved exclusively for us. He provided cover by telling other departments that his team was not available for tasks that were not tightly connected with our most important priorities. He infused fun into our day by getting together with the team and encouraging jokes and games and ordering food for everyone.

This extraordinary approach made us work harder and smarter and shine in front of the management.

About Making Your Co-workers Shine:

The best way to become a star in other people's eyes is to make them SHINE. Acknowledge their goodness. Praise their strengths. Extol their virtues. Compliment them for their efforts. Talk about their positive qualities with others. Make them feel special. Give them undivided attention. Help them reach their milestones. Celebrate their achievements. Empower them. Inspire them. Be there for them. Have fun with them.

Psychiatrist Edward Hallowell in his book *Shine* writes about the five-step process for peak performance, which he calls the Cycle of Excellence. The steps are:

Select

Connect

Play

Grapple and grow

Shine

Help colleagues figure out what they should be doing. Create an environment that is conducive for them to perform. Lighten up the mood with playful, creative and imaginative activities. When enthusiasm wanes, provide support and guidance till they achieve their goal. While celebrating the success of star performers, remember to nurture those still finding their way.

Be like the candle.

As James Keller said, 'A candle loses nothing by lighting another candle.'

Action Points

Create opportunities:

1. Delegate tasks that allow co-workers to showcase their skills.
2. Nominate them for collaborative projects.
3. Encourage them to speak on the stage at conferences or workshops.

Acknowledge:

1. Highlight your co-workers' contributions.
2. Recognize them through awards.
3. Publicly appreciate them.

Provide support for growth:

1. Mentor them.
2. Offer specific and actionable feedback.
3. Empower them.

Remember,

Sharing your light amplifies your own brilliance.

33

Manage Your Energy

And what is a man without energy? Nothing—nothing at all.
—Mark Twain

These two instances are from the time when I was managing a sales team in a bank in Mumbai. The first instance is about boosting individual energy and the second is about enhancing team energy.

I would often see Hari hit a mid-afternoon slump. But before that, right from the time he started work, up until the time his energy began to wane, he was full of vitality and vigour. One day I called him and said, 'Hari, go and take a nap for fifteen minutes.'

Too stunned to react, he started mumbling, 'Sorry, sir, I will go on a call now.'

'Go for the call after you have taken a nap. I am not requesting you. Consider it an order,' I said, and pointed towards an empty room next to my office. Reluctantly, he went inside. I called out, 'Sleep only for fifteen minutes.'

After the power nap, Hari was a transformed man. His energy was back to its high level. From the next day onward, incorporating this fifteen-minute recharge became a regular habit with him.

To enhance team energy, I introduced Fun-n-Frolic Fridays. After a tiring week, the team felt tired and down, so to lift their sagging spirits, I would tell them to gather in the open space in the branch and then all of us would sing and share funny experiences.

More than time, it is the energy that needs to be managed. My sales team did phenomenally well because of the steps that I took to restore their energy.

About Managing Your Energy:

Have you seen people coming to work in the morning with no energy at all? You wonder how these listless and lethargic people are going to last until evening? Such employees puncture the enthusiasm of those who are trying to be enthusiastic.

Energy is everything. It makes you alive. It lifts the mood. It pushes you, pulls you, elevates you. But only if this energy is positive. Negative energy can have the exact opposite effect. But here we are dealing with only positive energy.

We all have our own energy levels. Some of us are more energetic in the morning, some in the middle of the day and some in the evening. The key is to work around our energy levels. That's when we will be performing at our peak productivity. That's when we can do much more than what we would otherwise end up doing. So, know your peak energy level, and focus on important and complex tasks then.

Be passionate and dedicated but don't put in all your energy in one project because when your energy starts to wane, you will have trouble coping. Instead, pace yourself; this will keep you in high energy throughout the day.

Single tasking, taking mini breaks, having fun while working and distancing yourself from negativity and negative people are some more ways in which you can keep your energy levels high. An energetic employee can perform at the highest level and maintain the team's morale.

Through energy management, you will be able to enhance productivity, combat distraction and sustain output.

Action Points

Optimize your work schedule:

1. Plan your high-energy tasks strategically by identifying the times of the day when you feel most alert and focused.
2. Keep your workplace organized; discard clutter.
3. Take advantage of natural light by opening curtains and blinds and taking short walks outside during the break.

Know your expectations:

1. Understand what and how much you can accomplish during the day.
2. Use low-energy times for administrative tasks and/or emails.
3. Do not overburden yourself with unnecessary work, especially outside your designated hours.

Disconnect:

1. Set boundaries and stick to them, such as no disturbance during the lunch break.
2. Understand your internal clock.
3. Keep yourself away from electronic devices.

Remember,

When you manage your energy, you remain
clear and focused.

34

Be Persistent

No great achievement is possible without persistent work.
—Bertrand Russell

This story from Russian folk literature speaks volumes about the value of being persistent.

Two frogs fell into a pail of milk. Both tried desperately to jump out. But as the sides of the pail were slippery and steep, every time they attempted to jump out, they slipped. Still, they kept trying, but could not make any progress.

Seeing that there was no hope for freedom, one frog gave up, and stopped jumping. It resigned itself to its fate. Soon, it sank to the bottom of the pail and drowned.

The other frog was made of sterner stuff.

Despite the odds, it persisted. It was tired and worn out and its jumps were not getting any higher. It struggled, but kept jumping. Eventually, the milk began to thicken. Its persistent efforts had churned the milk into butter. Now, because of the thicker consistency, the frog was able to jump out of the bucket.

Its persistence had paid off.

About Being Persistent:

To achieve success, you must focus on your task. Close all doors so you don't escape. You will be assailed with self-doubt. Overcome it with positive self-affirmations. There is no going back. The only way is to forge ahead. Colonel Sanders approached 900 chicken shops with his recipe before it was accepted and the rest, as they say, is history. We all know KFC.

We can do anything. Believe me, anything. But we don't persist. We try doing it once, twice, thrice, maybe ten times, and then we get fed up and abandon it. Unless we keep pushing, keep trying again and again, keep persisting, success will elude us. Success is there waiting for all of us. But success will not come to you. Success doesn't need you. You need success. So, you must go to it. And it will be more than happy to welcome you.

Failure cannot touch you if you persist. Persistence is the enemy of failure and the friend of success. No journey towards success is smooth. Setbacks and struggles, falls and stumbles, obstacles and barricades, criticism and self-doubt, all these will make your journey as tough as possible. Many give up. They are unable to bear the pressure. But the handful of those who are willing to continue reach their desired destination.

Persistence is that one single quality that can make fortunes turn in your favour. So, if you want to SHINE at work, don't give up on the tasks and assignments that are allotted to you. Keep doing those despite facing difficulties and obstacles. *God helps them who help themselves.* So stick to it. There are thousands of stories that prove that persistence pays. Colonel Sanders's story is one. Jack London's is another. His first story was published after 600 rejections.

Persistence teaches us the value of success. It makes us consistent, and consistency is what people look for in the workplace because consistency means that you can be relied upon.

Therefore, persist, persist, persist. You will see the light.

Action Points

Develop strategic persistence and adapt your approach:

1. Engage in positive self-affirmations (write down and say an affirmation that helps you to move forward towards your goal).
2. Be patient and time your efforts; don't expect immediate results.
3. Read inspiring stories of people who have overcome obstacles and achieved their goals through sheer perseverance.

Develop your belief:

1. When things get hard, boring, challenging or painful, it's tempting to give up, but if you believe in yourself and your goals, you will continue. So deepen your belief by thinking positively and living it. Action is the key.
2. Regularly remind yourself that you are capable, worthy and good enough to accomplish what you have set for yourself.
3. Keep going, keep fighting, keep learning, keep finding ways.

Articulate your vision and be persuasive:

1. Break down your vision into manageable milestones.
2. Ensure that every action of yours is aligned with your vision.
3. Hone your convincing skills by building rapport and positivity.

Remember,

Peristence is the pathway to your desires.

35

Believe in Yourself

Believe in yourself. You are enough.

—Caroline Ghosn

6 May 1954. A historic day.

On this day, Roger Bannister proved to the world what can be achieved if you just *believe in yourself*. Before this, no human had run the mile in less than four minutes. Why was this so?

Many experts believed it was beyond the capability of the human body to run the mile under four minutes. Some even said that anyone trying to attempt the feat would end up with lungs that would explode, leading to certain death. Running a mile under four minutes was physically impossible.

But for Roger Bannister, this was never a barrier. His belief in himself was incredible. On 6 May 1954, he ran the mile in 3 minutes and 59.4 seconds. He not only created a world record but conquered the false belief that existed in the minds of other runners.

How long did Bannister hold this record? One would think that it should have endured for years. But no. Just forty-six days later, the record was broken by John Landy. Now, runners are consistently running the mile under 4 minutes. This became possible because the barrier had never existed. It was all in the mind.

About Believing in Yourself:

You can't create miracles if you don't believe in yourself. Only you can limit yourself. Don't be a stumbling block in your own way. If that stupid voice tells you that you can't do it, do it anyway. Shut that voice up. Don't let it dominate you.

Resist its alluring enchantment because it will lead to disappointment and regret.

Mohammad Ali once said, 'I am the greatest. I said that before I even knew I was.' Take a leaf from his book. Believe in yourself. Believe that you are made for greatness. Believe that you are a legend. Do not worry about haters. That's their job. What's it got to do with you? Do not worry about doubters. That's the way they are. What's it got to do with you? The moment you start believing, you will start achieving. The day you realize what your capabilities are, you will astound yourself more than others.

Don't wait for encouragement. If it comes, well and good. Don't waste time in waiting for inspiration. Get going. Get doing. It will come when it has to. Even if it doesn't, you would already have made plenty of progress. What you think of yourself is more important than what others think of you. Others may think you are super, but if you think you are not, you can't be. But if others think you are ordinary and you think you are extraordinary, then you can prove them wrong.

Listen to inspiring stories of great people. Read about miraculous accomplishments. But write your own tale of achievement too. Anything is possible. At the age of twenty-three, Jim Carrey wrote himself a cheque of $10 million and carried the cheque in his wallet wherever he went. He dated it ten years into the future and wrote it at a time when he was struggling to find a footing in the film industry. In ten years, he had become a superstar and was signed for a film for the same amount. Is this the law of attraction? I don't want to argue on it. Maybe it is. But because he believed in himself, the law of attraction worked in his favour.

Only when you believe in yourself will others believe in you.

Action Points

Challenge negative self-talk:

1. Act positive to get positive.
2. Create healthy routines.
3. Focus on what you are good at.

Embrace challenges:

1. Remind yourself that setbacks are a potential source of growth.
2. Consider obstacles as opportunities.
3. Don't dwell on mistakes; focus on progress.

Surround yourself with positive influences:

1. Eliminate negative influences that drain your confidence and energy.
2. Be with people who believe in you.
3. Listen to inspiring speeches and read motivating books.

Remember,

Your journey to success begins with self-belief.

36

Quantify Your Performance

An ounce of performance is worth pounds of promises.
—Mae West

Amal and Mahira were both vying for the position of Project Manager in the IT Department. Both had the experience, expertise and the technical skills required for the role. Both were exceptionally good and had the required soft skills. Both would have done justice to the role.

On the day of the interview, both appeared before the panel. Amal was able to show the panel a clear track record of all her deliverables, projects that she had delivered within the budget, every single milestone that she had achieved during the current year and the past one, written testimonials from other stakeholders, her manager and clients, praising her work. Mahira, on the other hand, was not able to provide any details about the way she had contributed to various projects. She only spoke about them.

Who do you think should get selected? The answer is obvious. Amal.

The reason is that she was able to convince the interview panel because she had quantified her performance. When you demonstrate your accomplishments in numbers, you leave no room for any doubt about your calibre and value.

About Quantifying Your Performance:

Put value to everything that you do at the workplace. Only then will you be valued. Otherwise, your work and effort won't carry much weight.

When you quantify your performance, your superiors will realize how valuable your contribution has been. And this value will benefit the organization.

You must express value in monetary terms or perhaps equate it to an FTE (full time employee). Time is money, so if your work/project/assignment is saving time, it's equivalent to saving money. Organizations attach a lot of importance to cost-saving, revenue-generating ideas. So, if you have such ideas, try to implement them and do the value calculation.

Never let your effort go waste. By quantifying, your effectiveness will get measured. You will know exactly what you have contributed and how much. In a race for a promotion, the employee who has a track record of projects delivered within the budget and deadlines and has written testimonials from clients stands a better chance than the one who has no record or evidence to show for their efforts.

Maintain a performance journal. Write down every achievement, however tiny it may be and every task/project that didn't get completed or was shelved. The time spent on them must be somehow quantified and shown to the appraisal manager at the time of performance evaluation.

Also remember to list all work done outside your KPIs (Key Performance Indicators). Those can make a huge difference in the final analysis. This includes tasks and contributions like voluntary work as part of your company's initiatives, CSR, presentations at seminars and conferences, capacity building that you were engaged in, collaboration with other units/departments, etc.

As management guru Peter Drucker said, 'If you can't measure it, you can't improve it.' So, measure your performance so that you can get better and better and thus SHINE ever more brightly at the workplace.

Action Points

Set goals and track your progress:

1. Define your key performance metrics.
2. Use technology to quantify your output.
3. Spend minimum time on (if possible, eliminate) tasks that cannot be measured.

Consider different types of KPIs:

1. Output KPIs to measure the tangible results of your work (e.g., reports completed, sales numbers).
2. Quality KPIs to track the quality of your work (e.g., customer satisfaction scores, error reports).
3. Efficiency KPIs to measure how efficiently you complete tasks (e.g., time spent on projects, completion rates).

Utilize data for improvement:

1. Benchmark best practices.
2. Analyse your data to identify strengths and weaknesses and act accordingly.
3. Data-driven decision-making will help you to prioritize your tasks and demonstrate what value you bring to the table.

Remember,

Your numbers define your value.

37

Think Big

If people aren't calling you crazy,
you aren't thinking BIG enough.
—Richard Branson

When you think this is my best, you can't think further. But every time after accomplishing something, if you tell yourself, this is not my best yet, then you can think bigger.

There are numerous examples of people creating wonders by expanding their vision. They simply did not know how to think small. They just thought BIG.

Oprah Winfrey rose from poverty to become a media mogul.

Stephen Hawking, despite his physical limitations, proved that intellectual pursuits have no boundaries.

Elon Musk has transformed areas of space travel and sustainable energy.

This applies not just to personalities.

Take, for instance, Dubai. The city that has no limits, no boundaries. From being a simple fishing village in the 1960s, it has become a shining example of a high-tech city that is expanding beyond imagination. It is the outcome of visionary leadership that believes thinking big is normal.

About Thinking Big:

You have only one life. Why waste it thinking small? Dare to dream. Dance with destiny. Reach for the sky. Then rest a while. After that, take another leap. Beyond the skies. There are many worlds to conquer. You are doing a great disservice to yourself by refusing to think BIG.

Thinking small will not take you anywhere. Do not suffocate yourself by stifling your aspirations and dreams. Widen your mind. Broaden your vision. Spread your wings and soar. You are somebody. Do not treat yourself as a nobody. There's a thin line between confidence and arrogance. Considering yourself as somebody is not arrogance, but confidence. But believing that *only you are a somebody* is arrogance. And if you consider yourself a nobody, then you are dead while you are alive.

How you perceive yourself is how the world perceives you.

At the workplace, it is equally important to think BIG. If you have set limitations that you will do only this much, that you will not go the extra mile, not take on complex assignments and are consistently afraid of failure, then you have a loser's mentality. Free yourself from this thought process. Liberate yourself by thinking BIG. Only then will you thrive.

The words and phrases that we use play a pivotal role in the way we think. According to David Schwartz, author of *The Magic of Thinking Big*, they either create small, negative mind images or big, positive mind images. So, choose your words and phrases carefully. They either reduce your stature or help you grow.

Action Points

Expand your horizons:

1. Allocate time to thinking (set aside fifteen to twenty minutes every day only for thinking).
2. Remove the word 'impossible' from your vocabulary.
3. Schedule time to explore the extraordinary.

Cultivate the belief that anything is possible:

1. Eliminate the use of negative words and phrases.
2. Practice assertive optimism.
3. Engage in 'What if' scenarios.

Set ambitious goals:

1. Push yourself beyond your comfort zone.
2. Create a vision board and represent your big dreams and aspirations on it.
3. Don't settle for anything less than outrageously big.

Remember,

Thinking Big is not just about what you want to achieve;
it's about an outrageously, bold dream,
the vision, the intent, the impact.

38

Use Words Carefully

Your words have power. Speak words that are kind,
loving, positive, uplifting, encouraging and life-giving.
—Unknown

Dr Jaikishen was a renowned surgeon, but he was also famous for being blunt. He was efficient in his interactions with his patients but lacked warmth. His patients always felt as if they were just numbers to him.

But when a young boy of about six or seven years was admitted for a critical surgery, Dr Jaikishen adopted a different stance. The boy was scared, and Dr Jaikishen could see it in his eyes. So, he deviated from his usual way of talking. He sat by his bedside and encouraged him to talk about his dreams. He used simple, honest, sincere words.

He assured and inspired him. Sometimes he said, 'You are strong and courageous.' Sometimes he said, 'You are a Superman.' And at other times, 'You are going to be all right,' and 'The post-surgery scar will be like a bravery badge for you.'

The surgery was successful, and the boy responded well. He remembered Dr Jaikishen's words all the time because they had a profound impact on him. Even Dr Jaikishen realized that healing is not only about medicine, but also about the way words are used. They can soothe or shatter a person.

About Using Words Carefully:

The way you use your words can make or mar your reputation. You can be seen as contemptuous, critical, quarrelsome and heartless or respectful, encouraging, agreeable and compassionate. Whatever we do involves words. Therefore, if we fail to use the right words in our communication, we won't get the desired results.

Whether at home or at work, we must get things done and to get our way, we should know what to say. We should be able to ask the right questions. We should be able to convey confidence. We should be able to negotiate. We should be able to convince. The way we use words shapes the influence we have.

You can be right, but not effective. You can deepen connections or distance others. You can achieve dramatically different results. You can make the listener feel pressured or relaxed. Your choice of words can sway people towards you or away from you. Phil Jones in his book *Exactly What to Say* writes, 'If you were to ask a room of a thousand people whether they considered themselves OPEN-MINDED, I am sure over nine hundred of them would raise their hands.'

At the workplace, if you were to use this phrase with a difficult co-worker, it could establish a bond between the two of you, or at least make that person feel more inclined towards you. For example, you can ask, 'Would you be open to working together?' This will engage collaboration. No one likes to be known as close-minded.

Put emotions in your words. Convey feelings with your words. Say what the other person would like to hear, not what you want to say. Include positive words in your conversation. Even when you are having a difficult conversation with somebody, do not allow negative words and phrases to be part of the discussion. Emotional vocabulary can make things easier.

To captivate audiences with your presentations or to persuade your boss to see your point of view, you need to connect at the emotional level. So the right type of positively emotional words can do the magic. Also, be a harbinger of good news. There is too much negativity floating around. As per Phil Jones, 'by prefacing things with the good news . . . you cause people to face forward with optimism and zap any negative energy out of the conversation.'

We can attract and repel people by our choice of words. Every word that we speak signals something about us to our co-workers. So, speak the right words to reach where you want to.

Action Points

Tailor your language:

1. Don't use those words for others that you wouldn't want to hear about you.
2. Use words that educate, empower and inspire.
3. Before speaking or writing, consider who you are communicating with and the situation.

Consider the emotional weight of words:

1. Certain words can have strong emotional connotations.
2. Avoid sounding harsh, dismissive or unprofessional.
3. If you can't make someone's day, don't spoil it for them.

Mind your tone and its impact:

1.   Be assertive, not aggressive.
2.   Use positive language always. Instead of saying, 'Don't be late,' say, 'Please arrive on time'.
3.   Do not raise your voice under any circumstances.

Remember,

> Every word that you utter can
> diminish or deepen a relationship.

39

Never Cheat

*We must remember that without integrity, nothing
else matters and that with integrity, nothing else matters.*
—Jon Huntsman, Sr.

Robin worked in a bank as an accounts clerk. He was a bright young chap with a rosy future. Once while facing a tight deadline, unable to handle the pressure, he opted for unfair means to complete his work. He knew about an automated script that could manipulate expense reports. To achieve faster results, he used the script.

He felt relieved that he had finished his task within the deadline but several days later, the external auditors found inconsistencies in the report. They remarked that the expense report was manipulated. Robin panicked. A big question mark hung over his future because he had shattered the trust placed in him.

His reputation was affected. His integrity suffered a massive dent. So massive that it could never be repaired fully. Disciplinary action was initiated against him, and despite his confession and his acceptance of full responsibility for his actions, he was suspended and his services terminated.

What could have been a flourishing career was ruined because of one single act of cheating. Robin's story is a warning for all of us. The temptation of a quick fix can lead to disastrous consequences. Trust gets eroded, reputations shatter and careers are finished.

Success is a combination of hard work, integrity and the courage to do the right thing, even when things aren't going right for you.

About Never Cheating:

The famous proverb *Honesty is the best policy* echoes a timeless truth. Whenever faced with a situation where you must decide between the right and wrong, think of this proverb.

Honesty is essential to moral character. Do you practice self-honesty as diligently as you project honesty to others?

Cheating makes you fall in your own estimation. The world may turn against you but if your conscience is clear, you can live. But if you are a cheater, the world may sing paeans in your praise, but you will suffer inwardly. Whether we accept it or not, we know the difference between the right and the wrong.

Everyone does it is a general excuse that people offer. *Cracked under pressure* is another classic justification. The phrase that we usually use, without realizing its implication, is 'at all cost'. I have to do this *at all cost* implies that you are willing to adopt malpractices in order to complete what you set out to. The right way is the only way. Tough, steep, full of obstacles, precarious, treacherous, thorny, whatever way you want to describe this path, do so, but take the honest path only. Jon M. Huntsman in his book *Winners Never Cheat—Even in Difficult Times* highlights an important point: 'Succeeding or getting to the top at all costs by definition is an immoral goal.'

Be competitive. Be fiercely competitive but don't resort to unfair means. Once you get stigmatized that you don't play and compete fairly, your reputation goes for a toss. Sophocles prefers to fail with honour than succeed by fraud. Stand out by being a person of integrity.

Action Points

Strengthen your values:

1. Understand your guiding principles to help make decisions aligned with your ethical compass.
2. Tolerating any form of cheating is cheating, so abstain from it.
3. Recognize your triggers to prepare healthy coping mechanisms.

True talent never cheats:

1. Make yourself a 'true talent'.
2. Never make excuses for poor performance (whether it is you or any of your direct reports).
3. Be transparent and seek help to overcome challenges, instead of resorting to dishonest means.

Build positive habits:

1. Develop a strong work ethic.
2. Have role models whom you admire for their honesty and integrity.
3. Stay committed to integrity by rewarding yourself for every temptation that you resist.

Remember,

Cheating is cheating. It doesn't matter
whether the dishonest deed is small or big.

40

Master a Skill

You must dedicate your life to mastering your skill.
That's the secret of success.

—Chef Jiro

What happens if you don't have mastery of a specific skill? You will never become the go-to person. You will just be one of many in the crowd. That doesn't serve the purpose if you are aiming to shine and prosper in the workplace.

Here's a story of Kiran and Javed.

Kiran worked as a salesman. But he did nothing to sharpen his skills. He often had to deal with foreign clients and thus proficiency in foreign languages would have not only helped him close deals but would have made him a master. He ignored language training offered by his company. Once, during a crucial negotiation with an important foreign client, he miscommunicated due to his limited knowledge of the language, which resulted in him losing the contract.

Kiran had a hard time explaining the mess to his seniors. He was moved out of the sales team to the despatch unit where he had to manage order intake and processing and communicate with field agents.

Javed was a graphic designer who stuck to outdated methods because he lacked expertise in new software and didn't make any effort to master it. As a result, he was unable to contribute in the right manner, thus hindering workflow and creativity. Soon, the company adopted a cutting-edge design platform, which further exposed Javed's limitations. He couldn't adapt. Deadlines were missed, colleagues got frustrated, and finally, the company had to let him go, hiring in his place a tech-savvy designer.

About Mastering a Skill:

Don't be a 'Jack of all trades'. It won't make you dazzle. I am not saying that the 'Jacks of all trades' are not worthy employees to have. They certainly do have their own strengths and advantages. They are creative and innovative and can draw connections from different areas of which they have knowledge. But being a master has its own advantages.

Be an expert, an ace, at any one skill. When you acquire mastery over something specific, you increase your indispensability at the workplace. You become a go-to person. You become a hero. A legend.

Without mastery, you will just be one of the many employees in office. Doing stuff, working hard, without getting any special recognition or appreciation. You will not have that extra edge which mastery will give you. Being a master will take you miles ahead of others. Your level of expertise will separate you from the rest.

An expert is an expert. The king of his domain. Your deep knowledge and experience will pull people towards you. Your opinion will carry weight. You will always be in demand.

In comparison to others, employers will be ready to hire your services at a premium.

Skilled in many areas or an expert in one. There is no right or wrong. Both career paths can lead to success. But to be a shining star at the workplace, being a master surely helps.

Action Points

Follow structured learning:

1. Choose the relevant skill that you are interested in.
2. Break the skill into smaller components.
3. Set yourself a goal.

Focus on deliberate and consistent practice:

1. Don't just repeat the skill mindlessly.
2. Dedicate consistent time to practising the skill.
3. Find someone you trust who has mastered the skill you are trying to master and take feedback.

Develop resilience:

1. As you master your skill, challenge yourself with increasingly difficult tasks.
2. Don't get discouraged by mistakes.
3. Maintain intrinsic motivation to fuel your persistence, through obstacles and roadblocks.

Remember,

You become a master when you raise
your passion to an obsession.

41

Navigate Office Politics

*To be successful in office politics, you don't have to be unethical
or play dirty, you just have to be aware.*
—Marie G. McIntyre

You can create opportunities for yourself if you know how to tactfully navigate office politics.

Let me share a story about Narendra Bhatia and Gaurav Kumar. Both worked in the marketing department. Both were eager to do well in their careers. But while Narendra faltered, Gaurav prospered.

Both had to meet their boss daily to discuss various issues. The gatekeeper to the boss's ear was Mini. But Narendra ignored her completely and would not listen to her ideas and suggestions. He forged ahead on his own, sidelining her. The outcome was that whatever proposal Narendra took to his boss was either declined or remained stuck.

Gaurav, on the other hand, was able to establish a solid bond with Mini. He gave her genuine compliments about her work and conduct, took her suggestions, paid attention to what she had to say. Whenever he went to his boss with proposals, he never failed to mention Mini's contribution.

Gaurav rose in the organization, while Narendra stagnated. Years later, a jaded Narendra, now reporting to Gaurav, who had become head of marketing, said, 'If only I had played the game wisely.'

'The game is not to be played, but understood,' said Gaurav. 'It's all about collaboration and not isolation. It's about taking people with you and not marginalizing them.'

The different approaches taken by Narendra and Gaurav in navigating office politics decided their fate.

About Navigating Office Politics:

If you are part of a corporate set-up, you can't rule out office politics. Where there are people, there is politics. Politics can be both positive and negative. You should know how to handle negative politics and play positive politics. After all, the workplace is like a jungle and only the ablest, smartest and the cleverest survive. The others either quit or hide.

Those who say that they are not interested in politics don't know that they are already a part of politics. You can't escape politics. You may not know how to manage and play it but you can't exclude yourself from it because then you get played by it. Navigating office politics requires skill. As Shiv Khera said, 'Office politics is the reason some people have jobs they don't deserve and some people don't have jobs they do deserve.'

You may know many people in the organization. But are they relevant? Also, do they know you and, if so, to what extent? Success at the workplace is not possible without this connection. You should know how to create an impression and on whom. Your advancement depends on your success rate in converting your foes into your friends.

You may be innovative, a go-getter and have brilliant ideas but your ideas may not get the green light. But another colleague may propose the same thought and get instant acceptance and approval. That's because he had more supporters.

Being a corporate worker is akin to being a chess player because office politics is like a chess game. You should be aware of the moves of others and know what move to make. Some good ways to play positive politics are projecting a professional image, volunteering, making yourself noticed, establishing a bond with key stakeholders, recognizing and praising co-workers for their contribution and helping them.

So, learn the game to shine.

Action Points

Raise your awareness and build relationships:

1. Observe the informal networks and power dynamics within your office.
2. Understand who the key players are.
3. Connect without an agenda and maintain cordial relations with everyone.

Maintain professional boundaries:

1. Mean what you say—be authentic.
2. Give people the benefit of the doubt.
3. Avoid gossiping and getting involved in personal conflicts.

Stay informed:

1. Keep yourself informed about important developments in office.

2. Don't spread rumours.
3. Focus on factual information and don't disclose confidential information to anyone.

Remember,

The office is a battlefield disguised as a workplace;
strategy is as important as skill.

42

Be Emotionally Intelligent

IQ gets you hired. EQ gets you promoted.

—Unknown

Some of the most successful and influential personalities in history have had high emotional intelligence. Be it Mahatma Gandhi, Martin Luther King, Jr, Abraham Lincoln or Nelson Mandela.

Look at Gandhi. He was of frail build and wielded no weapons. Yet, he derived his power from the understanding of the human heart. Facing the British empire was no easy task, that, too, without arms and ammunition.

His ability to empathize with the British was a key factor in winning the battle against them. Imagine empathizing with your enemy. We don't even do that with family and friends. Gandhi used his superior emotionally intelligent skills to understand the enemy.

He traded hatred with love, oppression with resistance, harshness with softness. He made the British see their own reflection in the mirror of non-violent resistance that he had created. He transformed his emotional intelligence into a scalpel, dissecting the very foundation of their rule.

This is not to say that Gandhi was superhuman. He also got angry and sad, but he didn't allow the anger and sorrow to trouble him. He channelled them strategically. That's the hallmark of superior emotional intelligence.

His tremendous understanding of emotions and knowing how to manage and use them to bring about positive change is a lesson for us.

About Being Emotionally Intelligent:

You may be intellectually superior to many, professionally much more skilled than your colleagues, and may have other traits and characteristics that distinguish you from them, but let me tell you, if your emotional quotient is average or below average, then you will face insurmountable problems.

Emotional awareness is the key to happiness and success. If you can touch someone emotionally, then you can get the best out of them. According to Warren Bennis, American consultant and author, 'Emotional intelligence, more than any other factor, more than IQ or expertise, accounts for 85 to 90% of success at work.' How you handle people in your day-to-day life at home and work determines how emotionally intelligent you are.

Connecting through the heart is more important than connecting through the mind, because the heart can change a person's mind. That's the power of having emotional intelligence. In Dale Carnegie's words, 'People are not creatures of logic but creatures of emotions.' So, in our dealings with them, our emotional quotient (EQ) plays a bigger role than our intelligence quotient (IQ).

If you are emotionally competent, you can handle pressure better because you will be able to control emotions and see reason. You can respond without reacting. Emotionally incompetent people crack, mess up, do not see reason and are reactive. The work environment suffers and thus productivity gets affected. An individual who can manage emotions effectively can produce great results, make the work environment fun and march ahead in their career.

Improve your emotional understanding to solve problems, make decisions and communicate effectively. You will encounter all sorts of people in the workplace, so you must be highly emotionally intelligent. Let me give you an example. Your boss may yell at you. His behaviour proves that he is not emotionally intelligent. You may yell back at him or start crying or get depressed; this shows that you too are not emotionally intelligent. The best response in such a case is to listen to *what* the boss is saying, instead of paying attention to *how* he or she is saying it.

Remember that everything is temporary. An irritating co-worker, a difficult manager, a pressing assignment. There's no point in getting worked up over them. Manage your emotions, instead of letting them manage you.

Action Points

Cultivate self-awareness:

1. Identify your emotions; that's the first step to managing them.
2. Understand and recognize how others feel; that's the second step.
3. Choose your responses, instead of reacting impulsively.

Develop emotional regulation skills:

1. Challenge negative thoughts.
2. Develop healthy ways to manage stress and difficult emotions.
3. Take breaks to help you regulate your emotions.

Strengthen relationships:

1. Put yourself in the other person's shoes before responding.
2. Validate others' emotions.
3. It's not only about you. Take the other person into consideration always.

Remember,

Whether you want to strengthen a relationship,
make better decisions or achieve greater success,
emotional intelligence does the trick.

43

Unlock Self-Awareness

I think self-awareness is probably the most important thing towards being a champion.

—Billie Jean King

A young man, known for his anger, approached a Zen master for help. He said, 'I have a quick temper and it's creating problems in my relationships.'

The Zen master smiled at him and said, 'I will surely help. Just demonstrate your quick temper to me.'

The young man stared at the Zen master, surprised at his request. 'Master, I can't do it right now. It happens suddenly.'

'Then what's the problem?' asked the Zen master. 'If your quick temper was part of your true nature, it would be present all the time. Anything that comes and goes is not a part of you, thus you shouldn't concern yourself with it.'

The young man took a while to understand what the Zen master said. Soon afterwards, he became more aware of his temper. This helped him to control it due to which he could have healthy relationships.

Becoming aware or knowing your point of awareness is a way to gain control over the emotions, beliefs and actions that were controlling you.

About Unlocking Self-awareness:

Daniel Chidiac in his wonderful book, *Who Says You Can't? You Do*, writes, 'Point of Awareness is the only spot that allows for maximum results and great change.' In life—whether at home or at work—you sometimes reach a point where realization dawns upon you. You become aware, your eyes open, you go into deep reflection and you start reassessing yourself. That's the watershed moment.

God opens other doors when one door closes, but we are focused on the closed door. Why did this happen? Why me? This is not fair. All these thoughts dominate our mind. We turn weak. We become angry. We stop being logical. But if we shift our focus from the closed door, a thousand possibilities will emerge.

So, at work, when a project fails or you are not given due recognition for your performance, it is not the end of the world. Know your point of awareness, as Chidiac says. When you know it, you can create magic. You can carve a new path for yourself.

The dead end is not really a dead end. The end is dead. You are on the threshold of a new beginning. A fresh start. The point of awareness makes you realize what your blind spots are. Once you know them, you will know what to do next and that's transformation because you have accepted the reality and are ready to change.

For Lao Tzu, knowing others is wisdom. Knowing yourself is enlightenment. How true is that! At that level, you are in a different state. Tasha Eurich, author of *Insight*, says, 'Research suggests that when we see ourselves clearly, we are more confident and more creative. We make sounder decisions, build stronger relationships, and communicate more effectively.'

Therefore, knowing your point of awareness is vital at the workplace.

Action Points

Do mindful introspection:

1. Start by self-reflecting.
2. Eliminate instant reactions/responses—always pause before taking action.
3. Examine your thoughts and beliefs.

Monitor your reactions:

1. Track your emotional triggers—notice situations, people or subjects that consistently elicit strong emotions from you.
2. Pay attention to your body language and physical sensations—clenched fists or a racing heart may indicate stress or anxiety.
3. Analyse your behaviour: is it aligned with your values?

Embrace different perspectives:

1. Explore the 'Why' in challenging situations. Ask yourself why the other person may feel the way they do, what they may be dealing with that you don't see, or why you feel differently than they do.
2. Take personality assessment tests to understand your personality traits and preferences, which can open opportunities for further self-reflection.
3. Broaden your self-awareness to discover hidden aspects about yourself.

Remember,

When you unlock self-awareness, you just don't start seeing, but are able to sense the unseen.

44

Seek Agreement on Your Priorities

The key is not to prioritize what's on your schedule, but to schedule your priorities.

—Stephen Covey

David was a good worker. He was focused and dedicated. Whatever tasks he had, he would prioritize them first, and then begin to tackle them one by one. All was rosy, until one day, his manager called him and asked him for an update on a project that was assigned to him.

David replied that he still hadn't started working on it because he was busy with other tasks. As soon as he finished those tasks, he would take up the project. He peered at the paper he was carrying and said, 'Sir, it's at number seven on my list.'

His manager who had so far been listening to him patiently, lost his patience, and said, 'This project is at priority number seven on your list. David, I had assigned you this project. It's number one priority for me.'

David was nonplussed. He didn't know what to do. He realized at the spur of the moment that all along he had been committing a blunder. He had been working on priorities that were his, not those of his manager.

His manager asked, 'Did we agree on priorities?'

'No, sir,' said David.

'Then how come you finalized on your own?'

'I understand now, sir,' said David. 'From next time onwards, I will make a list of tasks and then sit down with you to agree on priorities.'

About Seeking Agreement on Your Priorities:

Do work based on your boss's agreement, not how important it seems to you. Else, it will just be a waste of your time and energy.

You may face a situation where you are already working on a pressing assignment along with your usual work, and a new urgent project comes your way. Avoid deciding on your own which one to finish first.

List down your priorities and go to your manager. Tell him in what order you are going to tackle the tasks. Either he will approve or will make a few changes depending upon his or her requirements. Rewrite the priorities in the new order decided after agreeing with your boss and then work on them.

This is a professional approach, and it never fails because you and your manager are in sync. So as Stephen Covey says, 'The main thing is to keep the main thing the main thing.'

By seeking an agreement on your priorities, you set yourself for success. You will know what the main things are and in which order you have to work on them and your boss will be in the loop. A win-win situation for everyone.

Moreover, saying 'No' becomes easier. Anything that comes your way now, you can decline politely because you are aware of your focus areas. But if they were to come your way without you setting your priorities and obtaining your manager's approval, then you would not be able to say 'no'.

In Denis Waitley's words, 'Don't be a time manager, be a priority manager.' So, don't do second things first.

Action Points

Find common ground and negotiate:

1. Identify areas of agreement.
2. Negotiate trade-offs, because not everything can be a top priority.
3. Be transparent because transparency helps everyone to understand the rationale behind the prioritization.

Focus on collaborative prioritization:

1. Don't directly ask the requester (manager or anyone else) 'What's the priority?' They may say, 'Everything'.
2. Instead, give the requester the tools they need to help guide you. For example, you can say, 'I am concerned about the dependency of *this* on *that*. Which do you think should come first?' or 'Will it work if I deliver *this* on *this date*, so I can get *that* done by *that date*?'
3. Focus on the desired outcomes rather than specific tasks—this allows for more flexibility in approaching priorities.

Communicate clearly and build a consensus:

1. Periodically summarize the discussion and reiterate areas of agreement.
2. Take consensual decisions based on urgency, resource allocation and impact on the company's goals.
3. Document the agreed priorities.

Remember,

You should know your manager's priorities
because that's what should be among your top priorities.

45

Ask Questions

The wise man doesn't give the right answers,
he poses the right questions.

—Claude Levi-Strauss

The air conditioner hummed monotonously. Mona, a young loan officer responsible for verifying the loan applications, was working with her usual care and attention. Each click of her keyboard echoed the unspoken rule of the bank: follow the procedure, don't ask questions.

But her mind buzzed with several questions. She wanted to know why loans were denied to small businesses with innovative ideas, but approved for established giants with shaky finances? Her colleagues told her not to ask anyone such questions.

One day, when a frustrated farmer walked into the branch, demanding reasons for the denial of his loan application, she decided that enough was enough. The loan clerk gave the standard response, 'Your land value falls short.' She requested the loan clerk to show her the farmer's application. On scrutinizing it, she noticed something different—a focus on sustainable practices and potential for community upliftment.

She went to her senior and said, 'Mr Krishna, this farmer's proposal is promising. There's no reason why we shouldn't approve.'

Mr Krishna was a stickler for protocol. He said, 'The manual is clear, Mona. No need to deviate from it.' She shared her concerns with a senior colleague, who also advised her not to ask questions. But Mona wasn't convinced.

She researched sustainable farming practices and their economic impact. The data she had gathered convinced her that she was on the right track. Once again, she went to Mr Krishna and presented her findings to him. 'By approving this loan, we would be helping not only the farmer, but also the entire community,' she said.

Mr Krishna was impressed with the data provided and her reasoning and said, 'Mona, by asking the question "Why" you have proved that sometimes the best solutions lie beyond the manual.'

This incident sparked a change. Employees were encouraged to ask questions and blind adherence to the manual became a thing of the past.

If you don't ask, you lose the chance to bring about a change.

About Asking Questions:

New patterns are created in your brain when you ask questions. Asking questions is not dumbness. It is creative wisdom. By asking questions, you help your brain to access details and process more information.

We learn more when we ask questions. We get new perspectives. We get exposed to new ideas. We start thinking outside the box. We come to understand that our world is not the only world. That there are as many worlds as there are people in it.

You will never know all the answers. But you can have some good questions. Questions that can shake people.

Questions that make one think, reflect, meditate and wonder. Questioning leads to breakthroughs. And breakthroughs open doors to explorations, which lead to discoveries.

Never be afraid to ask. The timid and the weak don't ask. The bold and the courageous ask, without a care in the world. They are learners. They are seekers. They are restless souls who want to do something big and dynamic. So they ask and keep asking. They are not content with one or two answers. They want more. So they ask more questions.

We become more able, more capable, more intelligent and wiser when we initiate questions. Our thinking becomes more focused. Sometimes we wonder if the question that we are going to ask is the right question or a dumb one. Well, let it be a dumb one. That dumb question can open a discussion which could lead to solutions to some complex issues. Dumb questions lead to innovation.

Dumb is not stupid. *'What would happen if I chased after a beam of light?'* This was the question that led to one of the greatest scientific discoveries of the world, the theory of relativity. Albert Einstein says, 'The important thing is not to stop questioning.'

At the workplace, ask why you are doing what you are doing. That will lead to investigation and answers. Those answers could be in the form of process improvements, better turnaround times, enhancement in customer engagements and other benefits.

Ask and gain or don't ask and lose. The choice is yours.

Action Points

Be clear and concise:

1. Be assertive. State your intent properly and clearly.
2. Focus on the value proposition—highlight the value to get a positive response.

3. Adjust your communication style depending upon whom you are asking.

Pay attention to the timing and context:

1. Choose a time when your co-worker is not busy and can focus on your Ask.
2. Be mindful of your co-worker's workload.
3. Don't force your request.

If your ask is a request, follow the above action points. If your ask is a question, follow the below action points.

Prepare and target your questions:

1. Don't be afraid to ask questions—this can only come with practice.
2. Ask authentic and open-ended questions.
3. Tailor the complexity of your question to the audience's level of expertise.

Actively listen:

1. Pay close attention to the response.
2. Ask follow-up questions.
3. Watch out for unintended answers—sometimes the most valuable information comes from what isn't said directly.

Remember,

A timely question can unlock a bright future.

46

Handle Pressure and Be Patient

*People who pressure you usually deserve a 'no'. People
who are patient with you usually deserve a 'yes'.*

—Alan Cohen

Luke, a new intern, closely observed how things happened in the office. The manager would pressurize employees to work harder and increase their output so that the company's productivity would increase. He would allot extra tasks without first knowing whether the previous assignments were completed or not.

Luke was fascinated by Larry, his supervisor. The atmosphere in the office was tense and stressful. But Larry went about doing his job without showing any strain or pressure. One day, Luke asked him, 'Larry, how do you manage pressure and show so much patience when most of us are so stressed out?'

Larry smiled at Luke and said, 'I also used to get rattled at first, but over the course of time, I realized I was reacting, when actually, I should be responding.'

Luke nodded, his eyes shining like a child's when it is hearing its favourite superhero's story.

'Basically, I stopped reacting,' Larry said. 'I started responding. I understood that I cannot change what is beyond my control, but I can change myself, for I can control my behaviour and actions.'

'That makes sense,' Luke said.

'I am better organized. I prioritize stuff that I am responsible for, and I focus on the present moment. By making myself more self-aware, I can handle pressure, and I would advise you to do the same, Luke.'

Luke nodded in agreement. 'One more question, Larry. How come you are so patient with the manager? He is so obnoxious at times.'

'My patience is a result of my mindfulness, my sense of gratitude and my ability to reframe situations. Patience gives me more control over myself.'

'So you don't get angry when the manager talks to you in a disrespectful way?'

'The way the manager talks to me doesn't reflect upon me. It reflects on him. And yes, I won't lie to you. I do get angry and let me tell you, Luke, there's nothing wrong in getting angry. It is a normal response to a specific situation, but I don't lose my temper, and that's important.'

That day, Luke learnt some lessons that would stand him in good stead.

About Handling Pressure and Being Patient:

Know when to be patient. Know how to handle pressure. Know with whom to be patient. Know on whom to apply pressure.

Different situations will arise at the workplace. No single day will be the same. Some days will be smooth and easy, some will be wilder than a rollercoaster ride. You may be tested, stretched to the limit and sometimes you won't know how to pass the time as you will have nothing to challenge you.

Be patient and things will sort themselves out. Impatience creates complexity and complexity leads to stress. Patience is a great virtue to have at the workplace. It strengthens relationships, develops decision-making and makes you more focused. Learn to accept situations. Don't lose time, energy and sleep over things that you can't control.

Patience will help you handle pressure professionally. At the workplace, you can't get away from pressure. It will come to you in various forms. Your manager may be a bully, your team may underperform, your peers may be jealous of you, you may have fallen behind on your targets, I can go on and on. If you do not practise patience, all these issues have the potential to make you a mental wreck.

On the other hand, you should also know when to use pressure. That's also a skill. Frequently things don't get done unless pressure is applied. You must rouse the team. Yes, motivation and inspiration do wonders, but sometimes you must change the tactic. The team should not get complacent. Stress or pressure tactics work under certain conditions. Understand these conditions and then use that tactic. Tell the team that they are accountable; if there are rewards for superior performance, there are consequences for below par performance.

Patience and pressure: If you are bad at both, you won't be able to make much progress in your career. But if you know how and when to use both, you can quickly climb the corporate ladder.

Action Points

Manage time effectively:

1. Create a clear to-do list.
2. Schedule buffer time.
3. Delegate and ask for help, if necessary.

Focus on what's happening around you:

1. See through the eyes of others.
2. Identify your pressure triggers.
3. Adjust your attitude.

Practise relaxation techniques:

1. During stressful moments, do deep breathing exercises.
2. Schedule short meditation breaks throughout the day.
3. Tense and relax different muscle groups progressively to release physical tension associated with stress.

Remember,

You can handle pressure only if you are patient.

47

Be Not Afraid of the Chaos

Growth comes from chaos, not order.
—Rakesh Jhunjhunwala

Disruption is the mother of innovation. When routines get disrupted, innovative ideas emerge because one is then forced to think outside the box. The way Haider Abbas, the marketing manager at Ring-a-Tone, did.

A well-planned launch campaign for Ring-a-Tone's new phone had been hijacked by a viral meme, ridiculing its design. This had created an uproar in the department. Morale was down and everyone looked frantic and clueless as to how to control the seemingly uncontrollable situation.

Haider Abbas did not panic. All through his career, he had been known for his unflappable temperament. His eyes were sparkling with excitement, because for him, chaos meant creativity. He gathered his team in the meeting room and said, 'Why don't we swim against the tide?'

Everyone looked at Haider Abbas in disbelief. They couldn't believe what they were hearing. 'Why are you guys so dumbfounded? Am I speaking nonsense?'

'You mean,' Akshay, the technician, asked, 'Instead of fighting the current, we should ride it?'

'That's what I want us to do,' Haider Abbas said. 'My plan is to leverage the meme's explosive growth, turn the mockery into humour and showcase the phone's features in a light-hearted way. People will like it.'

He led brainstorming sessions in which he asked his team to take this as a game and come up with witty tweets. One after another, tweets were drafted, all addressing the meme head-on. Funny videos starring employees were made, and they even collaborated with the meme creator to design limited edition 'meme-ified' phone cases.

Within days, the situation was different. The narrative flipped. The negative became positive. The engagement with people became playful, the meme became a badge of honour, a shared joke between Ring-a-Tone and its audience. Pre-orders rose and kept rising, exceeding all expectations.

Haider Abbas had transformed chaos into a springboard for success. 'Consider chaos as a blank canvas,' he said to his team, when things were back in order. 'Paint it with your imagination and creativity.'

About Not Being Afraid of the Chaos:

Order is desirable, but don't fear chaos. Find stillness within the storm.

Chaos is an eye-opener. In chaos, you see opportunities. Chaos doesn't mean out of control. Anything that is out of control is risky. It could lead to disaster. Chaos fuels critical thinking. When you aren't aware of what to do next, you must force yourself to find a solution. Chaos can spark collaboration and engagement between employees. There's more team spirit and bonding. You get to learn more. Your skills for adaptability get honed.

Chaos looks scary because of its uncertain and unpredictable nature. But organized chaos could be just what the doctor ordered for your company in these unsure times. Too much structure and order kills creativity in the workplace.

Take the plunge but not without testing the waters. American educator and civil rights activist Septima Clark considers chaos as a gift. She says that whenever there is chaos, it creates wonderful thinking. And this wonderful thinking can make the workplace a hub of action and innovation.

Not everyone may enjoy working in a chaotic environment. Many would want to work in an environment of systematic order. There is nothing good or bad about either. Both have their pluses and minuses. Chaos is daring, adventurous, risky and exciting. Those who can adapt themselves to work in a set-up of organized chaos can shine with their creativity and innovative ideas.

Action Points

Develop adaptability:

1. Don't get caught up in a myriad of different actions and responses that only further perpetuate the chaos.
2. Know that there's no immediate answer to many things.
3. Be bold but not reckless.

Cultivate inner calmness:

1. Hang on; this too shall pass.
2. Practice mindfulness.
3. Trust your intuition.

Find strength in collaboration:

1. Be with supportive people who can offer encouragement.
2. Chaos can be easier to weather when faced collectively, so collaborate.
3. Have a clear vision when the path seems certain.

Remember,

Staying calm in chaotic situations helps maintain order.

48

Reinvent Yourself

People who cannot invent and reinvent themselves
must be content with borrowed postures, secondhand
ideas, fitting in instead of standing out.

—Warren Bennis

'Don't be afraid to reinvent yourselves,' boomed the voice of Vardharajan, a leading figure in financial technology. He was addressing a room full of young professionals who were bubbling with energy and excitement. They were devouring every word that emerged from the fintech expert's mouth. 'The world is changing and so must we,' he continued. 'Your most valuable asset is not your experience but your ability to learn and adapt. Let me share an experience from my professional life about how and why to reinvent yourself.'

He narrated the following story:

'I was known as the king of spreadsheets. For more than twenty years, I navigated the labyrinthine world of finance, my fingers danced across keyboards with the precision of a concert pianist, so good was I at my work. Everyone marvelled at my efficiency, and many envied my stability, and I . . . I just drifted.

'I became complacent, the spark in me dimmed and the tasks that I once found challenging stopped arousing my interest. "Is that all there is?" I would think. Around that time, a fresher, Madhav, joined. He was a bundle of energy and a whirlwind of creativity. He constantly suggested new approaches, questioned the set procedures and even had the courage to tell me that a tedious report that I generated monthly could be automated.

'I straightaway told him, like most of us do, that it was just not possible. But that night I couldn't sleep. I kept staring at the familiar spreadsheet and recalled Madhav's words that this could be automated. It dawned upon me that my skills that were once priceless were becoming obsolete, and that if I did not do something soon to bring about a change in myself, I risked being left behind. Automation was the future. There and then, I decided to reinvent myself.

'I began taking online courses, read plenty of books on automation, financial analytics and AI. It was difficult, at first, because the learning curve was steep but the thrill of rediscovering my intellectual curiosity made it worthwhile. In a few months, I presented the automated report to my astonished team. Madhav's eyes gleamed with respect.

'My reinvention not only renewed my skills and potential, but also allowed me to mentor Madhav and others. So, my friends, be bold, be adaptable, do not be afraid of change, but become a new you by changing yourself.'

About Reinventing Yourself:

If you stop challenging yourself, you are telling yourself to stop growing. Challenges make you throb with life. They make you eager and keen to push forward. Don't let yourself stagnate.

Whenever you feel you are not doing enough or you are stuck in a rut, instead of letting things drift and overthinking and getting stressed, REINVENT yourself.

But if reinventing was so easy, everyone would be reinventing themselves. The very thought of reinventing themselves makes people freeze. You can't unlock your full potential if you do not reinvent yourself. That's the surest way to dig deep inside yourself and open the door to the room in which your potential is imprisoned.

Reinvention is a journey, not a destination. It is the journey of self-discovery. When you decide to reinvent yourself, you take those crucial steps towards becoming different from others. You are about to move away from the herd. You are on the verge of rewriting your life story. You are ready to take the leap of faith.

Don't hold yourself back. Don't deny yourself the opportunity to become a legend. You are a star. And stars shine. So, you too should shine. When you shine at the workplace, you attract the attention of seniors and the senior management team. Those key people who can make a difference to your career growth. In these uncertain times, you must enhance your value.

Critically examine yourself, understand how you are perceived, determine the way forward, start the change in bits and pieces, take on new challenges, dare to be different. Start loving what you hate. If you are averse to digital technology, go ahead and learn something about it. Request your manager to give you a task outside your work area or area of expertise.

When you constantly accept challenges and are willing to go the extra mile and are ready to embrace difficult situations in life and work, you are in the process of REINVENTING yourself.

Action Points

Undertake a journey of self-discovery:

1. Practise self-reflection.
2. Ask yourself what you want to change.
3. Be honest with yourself.

Develop new skills and knowledge:

1. Identify your passions and values.
2. Invest in learning and development.
3. Practise and experiment.

Take control of your journey of self-discovery:

1. Build a support system.
2. Keep monitoring your progress.
3. Stay persistent and committed to your goals.

Remember,

> Reinvent yourself or become irrelevant.

49

Build Alliances

Alliances and partnerships produce stability
when they reflect realities and interests.
—Stephen Kinzer

Wayne Daniel was a brilliant programmer, often toiling alone. He kept to himself, preferring isolation to collaboration. His teammate, Rohan, on the other hand, thrived on collaboration. He reached out to people, built bridges across departments and established connections even with employees who were remotely placed.

When a crucial project came up, requiring both technical prowess and marketing savvy, Daniel, the obvious choice for the technical lead, was passed over. The manager, impressed by Rohan's alliance building efforts, knew he could unite the programmers and marketers, an effort which was crucial for success.

Daniel was stung by the rejection. He isolated himself further. Rohan tried several times to collaborate with him, but Daniel refused, coding furiously late into the night. But because Daniel worked alone, many essential requirements like marketing insights, remained inaccessible to him, due to which his code lacked user-friendliness. The launch deadline was nearing, and the team's morale was down.

Desperate, Daniel approached Rohan, who agreed to support him, even though precious time had been lost. The launch received lukewarm reviews due to its clunky interface. Wayne Daniel, once hailed as a prodigy, was sidelined and considered difficult and unapproachable. Rohan, however, thrived. He was recognized for his alliance building spirit and the ability to bridge the gap.

Ignoring alliances cost Daniel dearly. In the fast-paced workplace of today, success rarely blooms in isolation. Building alliances isn't just a feel-good buzzword, it's the key to success.

So, build bridges, share strengths and foster camaraderie.

About Building Alliances:

Allies in the workplace are an absolute necessity. If you are clashing with others, you are reducing your strength, increasing your problems and setting yourself up for failure. It's not only about having a great equation with your manager, but also with your team, peers and those who are not in favour of you.

Do not ignore anyone. You never know when someone can come to your help. Cultivate relationships by highlighting other people's interests and telling them how they can benefit. Everyone in the organization has different needs but they are all tied to you because of the organization's goals.

You may need information, feedback or good counsel from others, and they in turn may sometimes need information, feedback and good counsel from you. Connect and they will connect. Reconnect with those with whom you are disconnected.

Alliances are not casual work friendships. They are more than that. 'A problem shared is a problem halved,' is an old famous proverb. Forging alliances makes it easy for you to discuss critical issues. An ally will give you a patient hearing and guide you towards solutions.

Let's admit that we can't go far alone. In the corporate set-up, it is just not possible, however mentally strong and skilful you are. But if you have allies, they will come to your aid. All said and done, allies should be treated as equals, irrespective of their titles and positions. Resolve conflicts at once. Do not complain to your ally's senior.

Strategic concessions can foster strong alliances. By valuing your allies' perspectives, you increase the likelihood of their support for your initiatives.

When you build alliances, place more emphasis on

- developing the right working relationship
- embracing differences (rather than trying to eliminate them) and
- encouraging collaborative behaviour

You may be a superstar at work and be critical to the team's success but you, alone, cannot make a team. For the organization to succeed, everyone needs to put in their best. So have as many allies as you can and SHINE along with them.

Action Points

Cultivate trust and transparency:

1. Establish common ground by identifying shared goals and values.
2. Practise open and honest communication.
3. Demonstrate reliability and consistency.

Focus on mutual benefit:

1. Identify the need.
2. Define roles and responsibilities.
3. Develop conflict-resolution systems.

Invest in the relationship:

1. Schedule regular communication.
2. Offer help and support.
3. Be flexible and willing to compromise.

Remember,

By building alliances, you can unlock true potential . . .
because you turn 'me' into 'we'.

50

Be Self-Motivated

Obstacles can't stop you. Problems can't stop you.
Most of all, other people can't stop you.
Only you can stop you.

—Jeffrey Gitomer

Let's learn from some well-known sportspersons. How do they keep themselves motivated?

Lionel Messi says that his passion for the sport keeps him motivated through the most challenging times.

For Simone Biles, it is the internal desire for growth to redefine her potential.

Inspiring young girls is Serena Williams' way of motivating herself.

For Cristiano Ronaldo, it is setting challenging goals.

Naomi Osaka's motivational drive is to emulate the achievements of her idols, Serena and Venus Williams.

The thrill of competing and proving himself against his rivals keeps Rafael Nadal motivated.

For Michael Jordan, it was the thrill of visualizing success.

Acknowledging and celebrating small improvements motivate Novak Djokovic.

So, all the athletes have their own special way of motivating themselves. How do you motivate yourself?

About Being Self-motivated:

If you want to get by with doing the bare minimum at work, you can behave the way you want. Every morning, come to office, sit at your desk, quietly do what you are required to do, then leave. But if you are determined to do something worthwhile, something that can add to your personality and make you a legend, then in every situation, be self-motivated. If you can manage this, then nothing, nobody, can stop you from making progress.

Your manager or other external factors like a salary hike, bonus or promotion won't keep you motivated for long. Not only will you be depressed, but your feelings will also negatively affect others.

Self-motivation is contagious. Your positive energy can uplift your team and boost productivity. Become your own best advocate. Understand your strengths and weaknesses to maximize your potential. Know thyself to grow thyself.

You don't have to do anything extraordinary to be self-motivated. You only must keep doing ordinary stuff day in and day out.

Positive self-affirmations, staying away from negativity and the desire to excel should keep you self-motivated always. Know where you fit in the company's big picture. Be confident about your competency and don't do things just to avoid negative outcomes. Do them with the aim of accomplishing your goals. Discover your strengths and focus on them. Let go of what hinders your progress.

Self-motivation propels individuals towards consistent and exceptional performance.

Action Points

Fuel your intrinsic drivers:

1. Connect your actions to a meaningful purpose to ignite intrinsic motivation.
2. Be clear about your goals.
3. Use mental imagery to boost confidence and increase motivation.

Develop healthy habits:

1. Create a positive morning routine.
2. Know how to lift your spirits.
3. Change your environment whenever you can.

Try new things:

1. Practise the WOOP (Wish, Outcome, Obstacle and Plan) technique, pioneered by Dr Gabriele Oettingen.
2. Reward yourself for every milestone that you reach.
3. Practise self-compassion; don't be too hard and harsh on yourself. It's ok to be down sometimes, but not for long.

Remember,

> Self-motivation is the engine that drives life
> forward; without it, you're merely coasting.

51

Be a Popular Professional

Being a professional means doing your job
on the days you don't want to do it.
—David Halberstam

Most people generally hold the opinion that a true professional cannot be popular.

When I was working in a bank in the Middle East, I had a senior colleague who also thought the same. We would often discuss this subject. His belief was that a professional who does their job sincerely will not have many friends.

I would argue that if a professional does the following, they will certainly be popular:

- be approachable and friendly: engage in small talk, smile and show interest in others
- be a good listener and show empathy
- collaborate: share knowledge and expertise, volunteer and help others
- celebrate the success of others: display genuine joy at a colleague's achievements

- maintain professionalism: avoid gossip and negativity, and be respectful to all

Adhering to these five guidelines will certainly make you popular, even if you are a thorough professional. Popularity shouldn't be misconstrued as being everyone's best friend. It is about building a network of respectful, supportive relationships that is mutually beneficial to you and your colleagues.

About Being a Popular Professional:

Being popular is one thing. Being a professional is another. Popularity at the cost of professionalism doesn't make sense. A professional being popular is a rarity because popularity comes from a combination of professionalism, positive attitude and effective communication.

According to MTCT (Mind Tools Content Team), professionalism is a combination of eight core characteristics:

competence
knowledge
conscientiousness
integrity
respect
emotional intelligence
appropriateness
confidence

Being a professional is a tough task. Exhibiting professionalism at every stage of your career requires determination and dedication. You must maintain a positive attitude and communicate effectively. It takes years of experience to perfect such conduct.

Once it is established that you are a professional, how do you become a popular one? There are many ways. But how you interact with your co-workers is the single most important way. If you can comfort others with your presence, if you have mastered the art of listening and you are always encouraging and motivating with your words, and you have charisma then your popularity is assured.

Unleash your inner star and captivate your office.

Action Points

Become a go-to resource:

1. Build a strong professional reputation.
2. Offer help by guiding, teaching, mentoring and coaching.
3. Develop a reputation for delivering high-quality work consistently.

Foster positive relationships:

1. Display immaculate manners.
2. Be approachable and friendly.
3. Celebrate others' success.

Contribute to a positive work environment:

1. Be a team player.
2. Maintain a positive attitude.
3. Share your ideas, voice concerns constructively and be receptive to feedback.

Remember,

To be a popular professional, you should
connect, cultivate and collaborate.

52

Don't Get Offended

The final proof of greatness lies in being
able to endure criticism without resentment.

—Elbert Hubbard

A panel of discerning clients was examining Sapna's products. She was known for her sharp wit and meticulous designs. One client, after scrutinizing the clothes on display, made a sarcastic remark about Sapna's colour scheme. A jolt went through Sapna, and she could feel anger rising in her. She was about to retort, the words poised like a bullet on her tongue, but at the last moment, she chose not to.

She took a deep breath, paused and, instead of firing back, met her client's gaze with a calm resolve. Then she went on to explain in a very professional and measured tone about her artistic choices and the rationale behind selecting those colours. The client softened because of her composure and soon a constructive discussion took place between them, leading to a fruitful collaboration.

Imagine if Sapna had taken offense at the client's comment and succumbed to her anger, she would have lost the client and ended up derailing the project. Choosing not to take offense isn't about weakness, but about strategic strength and the ability to see the bigger picture.

Whenever you face criticism, do not react. Take a moment to compose yourself, listen to what is being said and ask clarifying questions. In the professional landscape, taking offense can prove to be a dead end. Always opt for understanding over anger and clarification over assumption.

About Not Getting Offended:

Those who aren't self-assured get offended with what people say about them. Uncertainty and insecurity about their beliefs and skills cause them to crumble the moment a negative word is spoken about them. Legends do not react to criticism in this way. They brush it aside and get on with their lives. They extract, from negativity, anything they find constructive and push themselves to become a more refined version of themselves.

I am not sure who said the following words, but they are usually attributed to Aristotle. 'Criticism is something we can avoid easily by saying nothing, doing nothing, and being nothing.' Even so, people will not stop criticizing. They will always have something to say. Focus on what matters, not what others think or say. Those who are poisonous will spew venom, regardless of our actions.

No one flogs a dead horse. Mediocrity is often cloaked in silence. The moment you dare to excel, however, you become a lightning rod. As your brilliance illuminates the shadows, envy ignites a chorus of critics, their voices growing louder with every step you take.

Do not let the critics know that their words or actions have hurt you. You are a star. Shine so much that you dazzle the eyes of your critics. Actor Channing Pollock says, 'A critic is a legless man who teaches running.' So, keep running. Keep achieving one milestone after another. There is no need to offer explanations or apologies, or to reason, argue, fight or take offence.

Ignore the noise, keep going.

Action Points

Practise emotional intelligence:

1. Don't react immediately in heated moments.
2. Train yourself to handle situations and behaviours that offend you the most by mastering your emotions.
3. Respond with compassion, rather than anger.

Set healthy boundaries:

1. Interaction is always a two-way street, so your efforts matter. Evaluate yourself before judging others or taking offence.
2. You have the power to choose—so if you don't like something that someone says, choose to ignore it.
3. Focus on the issue, not the person.

Assume positive intent:

1. Learn to give people the benefit of the doubt.
2. Don't jump to conclusions.
3. Don't take things personally.

Remember,

True power resides in elevation, not retaliation.

53

Compete Above Your Expertise

Don't limit yourself, discover new areas of expertise.
—Sunday Adelaja

Rakesh Parikh had a yen for numbers. His world consisted of spreadsheets and audits, far away from creative pursuits. But when he saw the poster for Design Challenge: Reimagine our customer experience, his competitive spirit was awakened. He heard his mind whisper, *this is not your cup of tea.* He ignored the whispers and signed up.

The room was abuzz with excitement. Experienced designers and artists with bold and colourful suggestions were discussing how they would shape their ideas. Rakesh felt lost; he had entered a completely unknown territory. But he didn't lose hope. He decided to link his strength to this entirely new area. For him, numbers were not merely cold figures; they held stories, patterns and emotions.

After office hours, he spent night after night, deciphering customer feedback and translating quantitative data into qualitative narratives. Finally, his concept emerged. He was thrilled. He had developed an interactive dashboard that transformed dry statistics into a visual journey of customer experience . . . it was not only informative, but also engaging and beautiful.

His data-driven narrative won the hearts of the judges. The trophy was proof that sometimes the most innovative solutions come from those who have the courage to compete beyond their perceived limitations.

About Competing above Your Expertise:

The consensus is that we should not compete with others because competing with others will make us bitter and depressed and damage our self-belief. However, if we compete with ourselves, it will make us better.

But what if we compete with those who are better than us? Benjamin Hardy in his book *Willpower Doesn't Work* writes 'Compete with those who are where you want to be.' Now, that's a solid challenge. If you accept it, you get an opportunity to learn and grow.

Many people compete with those at the same level. There's nothing much to gain in doing this. Compete above your level of expertise. This will add to your personality as a professional. It will give you that extra edge. Learn from the best to become better.

Competition sharpens our skills, makes us more competitive, adds value to our overall personality and creates an aura around us. Our focus shouldn't be on winning against them but on learning from them. When we see them in action, how they communicate, how they project themselves and how they run their business, we become inspired to give our best, stretching ourselves to the maximum limit, which otherwise we wouldn't have.

To level up fast, work with the best. Learn from experts, be inspired by their brilliance and watch your potential soar. Your next big leap starts here.

Action Points

Be agile, adaptable and innovative:

1. Know what you are up against.
2. Develop a competitive attitude.
3. Be ready to accept imperfections.

Collaborate strategically:

1. Partner with experts whose expertise is greater than yours.
2. Build strategic partnerships.
3. Develop a compelling value proposition.

Acquire knowledge:

1. Be realistic about your current level of expertise.
2. Create a focused learning plan.
3. Accelerate your learning curve by seeking mentorship/ coaching.

Remember,

Comfort is easy, growth is daring.

54

Be Curious

Replace judgement with curiosity.

—Lynn Nottage

Jeff Immelt, former CEO of General Electric (GE), credits curiosity for his career success. 'I spent a lot of time just seeking people out. That's how you learn. You've got to be the initiator. You must be constantly curious. You must see people when you don't need anything. That's one of the secrets of life.'

Immelt visited GE plants and factories around the country and walked around the factory floor, halting at stations to talk to employees and asking them questions like *What do you do, Why do you do what you do, How do you do what you do.* He never cared about whether he sounded silly or stupid. The learning that he gained from asking such questions, he said, was profound, and that was all that mattered in the end.

Below are some of the ways in which he championed curiosity and its impact:

- personal anecdotes: he shared stories from his personal experiences and referenced 'a relentless curiosity' as a key driver to his decisions

- public statements and writing: in his various speeches, articles and interviews, he argued that leaders need to be 'forever students' and that curiosity led to innovation and agility
- company culture: during his tenure, he instilled a culture of curiosity at GE. He encouraged employees to experiment, take risks and learn from failures

He promoted curiosity through six sigma, imagination breakthrough awards and an initiative known as FastWorks. His successful investment in renewable energy and the acquisition of healthcare companies were due to his focus on curiosity.

So, open your mind, be free and ask questions. What may appear to be a silly question could lead to a major breakthrough.

About Being Curious:

Climbing the corporate ladder demands a potent mix of brainpower, heart, hunger and passion. Curiosity, the catalyst for innovation, is the fifth essential ingredient for professional success.

People who lack curiosity rarely do well at work. A curious mind is a hungry mind. It keeps looking for ideas, innovations, new ways of doing things and is ready to experience the unexplored. Talent is common, but curiosity is rare. Most people have one without the other.

Curiosity leads to a new and exciting world. Many possibilities emerge. Outdated processes and procedures get challenged by a curious workforce. The organization changes, and change is always good. A mindset of 'Can't' gets replaced with 'Can'. New ideas, new efficiencies, new look, what can curiosity not lead to?

The best way to connect with reality is through curiosity. Do not confuse curiosity with nosiness. Being nosy involves prying into other people's affairs; you want to get to know something about them which you can use against them for your personal gains. Being curious means wanting to learn, to know more, to seek knowledge.

At the workplace, if you exhibit the trait of curiosity, you will have improved job satisfaction and performance and be creatively enhanced. If you want to stay ahead of the game, focus on your curiosity. Enquire, read, ask, investigate, discuss, take feedback, open your mind.

Think of optimizing processes, research customer preferences, visit your competitors and see how they function. Spend time in self-analysis. Don't just do something because it is an accepted practice. Growth, innovation, success, they all come if you show curiosity.

Brian Grazer, in his book *A Curious Mind,* writes, 'More than intelligence or persistence or connections, curiosity has allowed me to live the life I wanted.'

Don't we all want to live the life we want? Being curious is the answer.

Action Points

Do things differently:

1. Practise some 'randomness' every day (for example, take a different route home from the office one day or spend time learning a few words from a unknown language).
2. Observe people and their mannerisms.

3. Visit other departments and units in your company and talk to the staff to understand their way of working and functioning.

Engage in playful learning:

1. Turn daily activities into explorations.
2. Find joy in discovery—take pleasure in the process of figuring things out.
3. Expose yourself to a wide range of ideas.

Be comfortable with the unknown:

1. Don't accept things at face value.
2. Move beyond 'yes' or 'no' questions.
3. View confusion as a natural part of the learning process.

Remember,

Curiosity isn't about seeking answers,
but imagining possibilities.

55

Know When to Say 'Yes' or 'No'

*The difference between successful people and
really successful people is that really successful
people say no to almost everything.*
—Warren Buffett

My life changed the day I realized the importance of saying 'no'. Like many of you, I would never say 'no' whenever I was assigned projects, assignments or tasks or when a colleague requested me for help.

I just kept saying 'yes' to everything that came my way due to which my days were a blur of tasks, deadlines and requests, leaving me tired and cranky. One day, suddenly, something in me snapped.

Arvind, a colleague of mine, with whom I shared cordial relations, requested me to complete a sizeable task as he had to go on a vacation which was planned months ago. My head buzzed with the familiar 'Yes', but this time, I could hear the whisper of another voice, a voice that I had never heard before. It was a tired, frustrated voice that said 'Enough is enough.'

I was already overburdened with work and this request felt like the proverbial straw that broke the camel's back. I said, 'No, Arvind, I can't do it.'

There was a pin-drop silence on the other side. Arvind, even in his wildest imagination, would never have thought that he would hear a 'no' from me. It was the turning point in my life and thereafter I had no problem saying 'no' to things that I knew were either irrelevant or not urgent or just being pushed on me or had nothing to do with my top priorities.

By learning to say 'no', I also understood the importance of saying 'yes' to the right stuff. From a chaotic rush, my life had a more intentional flow. I was more in control and the quality of my work and productivity increased.

I admit that it wasn't easy. At times, I experienced moments of guilt, fear of judgement and pressure to conform, but with each 'no', I grew stronger, more confident in my boundaries and priorities.

My 'no' became a powerful tool for redirection.

About Knowing When to Say 'Yes' or 'No':

Saying 'yes' is easy. Saying 'no' is challenging. But as a professional, you should know how to say 'no', and, when. You set boundaries when you say 'no'. Greg McKeown, author of *Essentialism* writes 'If you don't set boundaries, there won't be any. Or even worse, there will be boundaries, but they'll be set by default—or by another person—instead of by design.'

Your 'no' raises the standard of your 'yes'. People go on saying 'yes' to everything without realizing what they are doing. They don't want to hurt people—my question is what sort of people are these who get hurt by your 'no', if it is a genuine one? You should distance yourself away from them. They don't mean well for you. Another reason for not saying 'no' is that they feel pressured; they just cannot say 'no' to that person because of a dominant personality, overwhelming presence, bullying nature, senior position or simply because all their lives they have just been saying 'yes'. So, saying 'no' doesn't occur to them.

In the workplace, you have your own tasks and deadlines to which you are committed. You also know that emergencies can come at any time, such as an urgent request from your boss or superior or getting assigned to a project which the senior management is backing. In this scenario, if your colleague asks you for support or requests you to do something, what should you do? The colleague may be close to you or may be a dominant person who has always been asking you for your support. You have never said 'no' and despite your busy schedule and knowing that you will have a difficult time managing this, you still say 'yes'.

You can't be effective if you always say 'yes'. And we say 'yes' because we want to help or feel productive or want to protect our reputation of being nice. We may even be scared or think that saying 'no' is a weakness. In such situations, you should be honest and straightforward. Put across your point politely but firmly and, without having to explain yourself, close the matter by saying 'no'. Be as transparent as possible, so that your colleague knows that it is not personal. Do not make anything personal in the office.

By adopting the practice of saying 'no', you get the right things done. You stay in control of your time and hence your work. If you allow your time to be hijacked by others, you will be struggling all the time.

The sky will not fall if you start saying 'no'. You will make a reputation for yourself by forming this habit. But always ensure that your 'no' is a required 'no' and not an excuse.

Action Points

Consider long-term impact:

1. Think before saying 'Yes' or 'No' (being strategic is the key).
2. Match your 'Yes' or 'No' with your career goals.
3. Your 'Yes' or 'No' should be aligned with your values and goals.

Identify potential conflicts:

1. Check your existing priorities before you decide.
2. Don't respond under pressure; take time to evaluate.
3. Your 'Yes' shouldn't push you to say 'No' later because of your prior commitments, on the other hand, your 'No' could become a 'Yes' later, if you deliver on your commitments earlier.

Use your fear and comfort zone as the guide:

1. Ask yourself 'Which is harder?'—'Yes' or 'No'.
2. The response that pulls you out of the comfort zone is likely to be a better choice.
3. 'No' is about focus and depth. 'Yes' is about giving yourself a chance.

Remember,

> Saying 'yes' has a price; a well-placed
> 'no' might be more valuable.

56

Find a Mentor

A mentor is someone who sees more talent and ability within you,
than you see in yourself, and helps bring it out of you.
                                                      —Bob Proctor

Stephen Davis knew that mentors, whether personal or professional, can make a huge difference in your life. He was a senior manager in a bank and aimed to reach the pinnacle. The first thing that he did was to seek out someone from the leadership team whose role aligned with where Davis saw himself in the future. He was a seasoned banker with his sights set on the top. A firm believer in the transformative power of mentorship, he initiated his ascent by identifying a senior leader whose role mirrored his career aspirations. He connected with Mark Robinson, the Chief Operating Officer, and requested him to be his mentor.

He immersed himself in understanding Robinson's leadership approach, meticulously studying his decision-making patterns. Eager to gain first-hand insights, Davis sought permission to observe Robinson's meetings, training sessions and public appearances.

When Robinson gave him constructive criticism, Davis accepted it without allowing his ego to come in the way. He realized that a good mentor was obliged not only to commend the positives, but also to highlight the areas that need improvement.

He learnt from the mistakes that Robinson had made. He asked lots of questions and soaked up the responses like a sponge. Using Robinson's connections, he established new relationships and built upon them and found opportunities to capitalize on. He understood from Robinson what worked for him and implemented the same tactics.

What you can learn from a mentor is invaluable. So, find a mentor, now.

About Finding a Mentor:

If you wish to improve your self-confidence and self-awareness, and increase your chances of securing a promotion and gain more insights that are relevant to your situation, find a mentor.

Anyone whom you consider a role model could be your mentor. Approach him or her directly if mentoring system is not in your organization. Share your aspirations and expectations with them and try to gain as much as you can from their experiences and expertise.

The influence that a mentor can have on your career can be a game changer for you. You can aim for greater success with their guidance. Their wisdom and command over their work will teach you what no books or training sessions can. A mentor is a catalyst for career growth, providing invaluable guidance on networking, feedback and effective communication.

As J. Loren Norris says, 'If you cannot see where you are going, ask someone who has been there before.' Practical knowledge and inputs from your mentor can put you in the driver's seat at work.

A mentor is your ally, your support system, your comfort zone, your teacher. Having a mentor at the workplace can transform your career and make you a solid professional.

For self-confidence, self-awareness, job satisfaction, aspiration, likelihood of promotion and fulfilment at work, seek a mentor.

Action Points

Identify potential mentors:

1. Target mentors whose expertise aligns with your aspirations.
2. Explore the networks at your workplace.
3. Reach out to someone you admire in the organization and ask for an introductory meeting.

Connect genuinely:

1. Get to know them.
2. Be grateful.
3. Be clear about your expectations.

Build the relationship:

1. Give value in return—consider what you can offer your mentor, because a connection with a mentor is a two-way street.

2. Respect their time.
3. Show initiative and take ownership.

Remember,

Beyond the lessons learned from personal trials, a mentor provides invaluable theoretical understanding.

57

Be a Mentor

Teach them the quiet words of kindness, to live beyond
themselves. Urge them toward excellence, drive them toward
gentleness, pull them deep into yourself, pull them upward
toward manhood, but softly like an angel arranging clouds.
Let your spirit move through them softly.

—Pat Conroy

Once upon a time, Maha, a fresh college graduate, stepped into the bustling world of corporate offices. The fluorescent lights, the hum of printers and the constant chatter—it all felt overwhelming. She was like a small boat caught in a storm, unsure of her direction.

Maha's lack of confidence gnawed at her. She questioned her abilities, wondering if she truly belonged in this fast-paced environment. The thought of quitting crossed her mind more than once. But deep down, she knew she wanted to thrive, not just survive.

And then, like a beacon in the fog, Nadya appeared. Nadya was an experienced colleague—a seasoned professional, who had weathered countless storms herself. She saw something in

Maha, perhaps a reflection of her own early struggles. Without hesitation, Nadya extended her hand in mentorship.

Their interactions were like sunlight breaking through clouds. Nadya patiently shared her knowledge, insights and battle scars. She taught Maha the unwritten rules—the ones textbooks don't cover. She showed her how to navigate office politics, how to communicate effectively and how to balance ambition with humility.

But it wasn't just about practical skills. Nadya listened when Maha poured out her fears. She encouraged her when self-doubt threatened to drown her. And slowly, like a sapling reaching for the sky, Maha grew. She gained confidence, not because she suddenly knew everything, but because she had someone by her side—a mentor who believed in her.

Nadya's impact rippled beyond Maha. As Maha blossomed, she became a source of inspiration for others. She paid it forward, helping new hires find their footing.

Mentorship isn't just about career advice or networking. It's about humanity. It's about lifting each other up, especially when the path seems steep. It's about saying, 'I've been there, and you can overcome this too.'

So, let's all be Nadyas. Let's extend our hands to those finding their way—the recent graduates, the fresh faces, the uncertain hearts. Let's share our knowledge, our stories and our encouragement. Because in doing so, we don't just change careers; we change lives.

About Being a Mentor:

The best way to increase your knowledge is to be a mentor. Mentoring can help move your career in the right direction. If you have the required knowledge, experience and mastery over a skill or two, you should volunteer as a mentor.

You can guide, advise, support and give feedback as and when required. You will get to play different roles, viz., role model, teacher, counsellor, advisor, advocate and ally. You will enhance your interpersonal skills and help the mentees to accomplish their goals. That will be an achievement.

Decide on a schedule, meet regularly, conduct yourself professionally and teach by example. Mentoring is all about engagement. As you start engaging with your mentee, you will be able to recollect the aspects of your profession that you like. You will experience a sense of fulfilment.

Moreover, it will be a learning opportunity for you. Whatever your experience may be, the mentee will also have insights into the latest trends and practices, making it a learning opportunity for you. You could add the mentoring experience to your CV, which will enable you to distinguish yourself.

Be clear, communicate well and stay committed during the mentoring period. Even if your organization doesn't have a mentoring programme, you can do it on your own. There will be a lot of newcomers in the company or juniors in your own team who can benefit from your mentoring, so mention that you are willing to mentor them. Involve your manager and HR also.

This initiative can create many opportunities for you inside and outside the organization. It is a win-win situation for everyone, the mentor, the mentee and the company.

Action Points

Empower and guide; don't dictate:

1. Let your mentee make their own decisions.
2. Be open about your own mistakes.
3. Guide your mentee to discover solutions themselves.

Ask powerful questions:

1. Ask questions that encourage critical thinking and problem-solving skills.
2. Use probing questions to uncover underlying issues and perspectives.
3. Use phrases like 'What if?' or 'Have you considered the opposite viewpoint?' to spark creative thinking.

Bring the mentees out of their comfort zone:

1. Don't babysit them.
2. Encourage them to take intelligent risks to expand their skill set.
3. Connect them with resources and network.

Remember,

Mentoring offers a unique opportunity for lifelong learning, as the act of teaching often illuminates new perspectives and knowledge.

58

Set High Standards

A person with low standards will forever be walking.
A person with high standard will soon stop walking and
start running. Later, they'll soon stop running and start galloping.
The next time you see him, he's either flying or soaring.

—Israelmore Ayivor

To inspire others and create a powerful impact, you must raise the bar. Set high standards for yourself. The way Monica, a calligrapher, did.

Surrounded by masters renowned for their flowing characters and intricate brush-strokes, she felt both inspired and intimidated. Yet, she never succumbed to self-doubt. She was determined to master calligraphy but that wasn't enough for her. She set an audacious goal for herself, to infuse her art with a unique blend of tradition and modernity. She wanted her art to reflect her own spirit.

While her peers copied the established styles, Monica experimented with unconventional methods and tools. She practised on unconventional surfaces like weathered wood, windswept sand, even petals of cherry blossoms. Her unconventional approach drew criticism. Masters scoffed. They said, 'Calligraphy isn't meant for experimentation.' But this did not deter her.

She had set her standards high and was not willing to compromise on it. As the wheels of time rolled on, her unique style blossomed, and gradually the whispers of disapproval turned into murmurs of admiration. One day, a famous art collector came across Monica's work. So captivated was he by her creations, he commissioned her for a special exhibition. Her name and fame spread. Her unconventional masterpieces started fetching record prices.

Monica's story is not only about artistic success but also about her refusal to settle for mediocrity, her willingness to challenge the conventional and her courage to raise the bar.

About Setting High Standards:

You should set your sights high. Be a cut above the rest. Do not ever think of lowering your standards just because others can't meet them. As Coco Chanel says, 'Don't be like the rest of them, darling.' Let others raise their standards to match yours. The one who lifts others is always on a higher level. Setting high standards for yourself is a way to push yourself to the maximum limit.

Raise the bar and keep raising it. Whether you are being watched or not, whether you are at home or in office, whether you are in a paid or free position, whether you have a title or not, whatever the situation strive for high standards. By aiming high, you become a catalyst for others' success.

On the flip side, you may find yourself alone because others are not able to match up to the kind of standards that you have set for yourself.

Don't let anyone judge you or tell you what you can or cannot do. You are the best judge of yourself and your capabilities. Having a high standard doesn't mean you are arrogant or snobbish, rather, it means you have an understanding of what you deserve. Simple and sweet.

Action Points

Define your values and goals:

1. Decide what you want to change about your work situation.
2. Determine outcomes and actions.
3. Embrace challenges.

Develop a continuous learning mindset:

1. Don't settle for mediocrity.
2. Seek continuous improvement.
3. Actively seek feedback from colleagues.

Practise self-discipline:

1. Develop a system to track your progress.
2. Know that if it must be done, it has to be you.
3. Be consistent, always.

Remember,

Good is the enemy of great. Don't settle for good enough.

59

Defy the Odds

Success is not measured by what a man accomplishes, but by the opposition he has encountered and the courage with which he has maintained the struggle against overwhelming odds.
—Charles Lindbergh

Marie Curie's life embodies the triumph of defying the odds in the male-dominated world of science. She carved a niche for herself, defying expectations at every turn. She had limited opportunities to study in Poland, the country where she was born in poverty. So, she moved to Paris, where she worked as a governess and did other odd jobs to pay for night classes at Sorbonne University. Being passionate about Physics and Mathematics, she went on to become the first woman to earn a doctorate in France.

There was societal scepticism and prejudice against female scientists, but she didn't let it affect her. She kept publishing groundbreaking papers and, in the process, became the first woman to win a Nobel Prize in 1903. Undeterred by sexism, she became the first person to win a second Nobel Prize, in 1911. She faced discrimination, limited funding and health hazards, but she never gave up.

From overcoming poverty and gender barriers to risking her health for scientific advancement, she shattered glass ceilings and paved the way for future generations of female scientists.

So, when you are faced with the odds, go ahead and defy them.

About Defying the Odds:

Defying the odds starts with you. Stop thinking that you are average. That's the first step.

Success is waiting for you. But it won't come to you. Just as when you are hungry, food doesn't come to you. Or when you are thirsty, water doesn't come to you. You must take action. You must go and eat food or go and drink water. In the same way, you must move towards success by taking the necessary actions.

Along the way, you will encounter odds that will make you want to give up and go back, but you must keep defying them, if you want to embrace success. Keep believing that you deserve good things. Brush aside the fears. Build a support system.

Self-belief is what puts you on the path to success. Once the decision is made, you have to bid goodbye to all your fears. If fear is your companion, you can't achieve success. Finally, the right people should be around you to help and guide you. In spite of taking all these steps, you will be tested. Self-belief is the cornerstone of success. It's the unshakeable foundation upon which dreams are built. Fear is the architect of doubt, a formidable foe that must be vanquished. Surround yourself with those who ignite your potential, and remember, every triumph is preceded by trials.

By defying the odds, you will be able to make things happen. You can choose to be a hero or a zero. That choice is entirely yours. Start right away by defying the odds. Identify the behaviour that you want to change, zero in on the preferred behaviour that you want to practise and implement. Apply the same logic in your workplace. Is there any process or procedure that you want to change or implement? See what the odds are and challenge them.

High-performance requires mental toughness. Either chicken out or follow your desire. The difference between ordinary and extraordinary is defying the odds.

Action Points

Cultivate resilience:

1. Identify a behaviour or process that you want to defy.
2. Find out the preferred behaviour or process that you want to practise.
3. There is no such thing as 'try'—either do it or don't.

Be resourceful and creative:

1. Think outside the box because defying the odds often requires an unconventional approach.
2. Leverage your resources creatively to your advantage.
3. Partner strategically with key players.

Keep believing in yourself:

1. *'Yes, I can!'* should be your mantra.
2. Be courageous; know that courage is not the lack of fear, but acting in the face of fear.
3. Stay focused.

Remember,

Either let limitations define you or you define
what it is to be limitless by defying the odds.

60

Know Your Peers

If you look to lead, invest at least 40% of your time managing yourself - your ethics, character, principles, purpose, motivation, and conduct. Invest at least 30% managing those with authority over you, and 15% managing your peers.

—Dee Hock

Ravie Khanna never treated his peers as rivals. For him, we were all his allies. He solidified peer relationships by making time for small talk. For five or ten minutes once or twice a week, he would drop into my office, after first checking with me if I had time to spare. Then, he would ask me about what's happening in my life, which book I was currently reading, and other small talk. He would do this with all his peers.

He always engaged in friendly chatter before or after the meetings that we would attend together. Ravie forged solid connections by keeping his word always. So, if he promised to do a task by a specific timeline, he would deliver. He was genuine in his praise. I still remember that he would always compliment me about my writing skills or about the way I had dealt with a tricky situation.

He never judged anyone, preferring to give the individual the benefit of the doubt. The one thing that really stood out in him was his ability to listen actively. This habit of his helped him learn about his peers. He knew more about us than our managers did.

He was ready to help and support us and used to go out of his way to do it. We too would reciprocate in the same way when he needed guidance and direction on some issue or project. This give-and-take approach drove the team's success.

By knowing his peers, Ravie was able to perform at a superior level. So, if you want to create an impression, make your peers your friends. Know your peers so well that they become your strength.

About Knowing Your Peers:

Your abilities matter. But beyond them, your understanding of your peers matters a lot. Their management is crucial for your success. You should therefore know how they operate.

Talent, competency, positivity, none of these will work in your favour if you do not know how people think and what their motives are. Differences between peers are bound to emerge because of different thought processes, mindsets, ways of looking at things, approaches towards problems, etc. Overlooking these challenges would hinder your professional development.

Maintain cordial relations with all of them, irrespective of what kind of signals you are getting from them. Your peers could be negative and positive. Some will genuinely like you, and some will fake it. Some will be supportive, some will just speak insincere words and some will simply not pay any attention to you. Do not sever relations with them. You never know when you have to work together on a project or they get promoted and you have to report to them. Then the situation will become awkward.

Managing up shows how effective you are at dealing with seniors and managing down displays how good you are at handling juniors. But managing peers is equally important, though it is not given that much attention. In 360 degree assessments, peer comments play a vital role in influencing the management's opinion about you. Most often, their feedback will be constructive and not flattering.

Peers are an important source of information and knowledge. They all have different connections. You may not know whom they know. Information and influence carry value in the workplace. If you establish a bond with them, they can guide you and help you to get out of sticky situations. They can also make things work in your favour by influencing the managers of other departments. Therefore, don't let misunderstandings occur between you and your peers, and if they do, tackle them immediately.

Action Points

Break the ice:

1. Keep your ego aside; there should be no ego if you want to learn from your peers.
2. Peers can help you to know what to do and what not to do—both positives and negatives.
3. Be personable, yet professional.

Engage in collaborative work:

1. Working together on a project will help you to know your peers' strengths, work styles and personalities.

2.   Offer them help and support.
3.   Show appreciation and acknowledge their efforts.

Show interest in them:

1.   Practise active listening.
2.   Ask open-ended questions.
3.   Remember details and follow up on personal interests or events they have shared with you.

Remember,

Robust peer relationships are essential for career advancement.

61

Reframe the Disaster

The true test of character is how we handle the little disasters in life.
—Sarah Vaughan

When I was managing a sales team in a bank in India, my boss, Chetan Sharma, reframed a disaster with his quick thinking and swift action.

The senior management team was assembled in the conference room, anticipation thick in the air. Chetan, the architect of a months-long project, stepped up to the podium. The room hushed in expectation. Then, the unthinkable happened. As he began his presentation, the screen erupted into a chaotic display of pixels. A ripple of laughter broke the silence, quickly swallowed by a wave of awkwardness.

I saw Chetan, a worried frown on his face, grab a tissue and wipe the sweat beads that had formed on his forehead. When everyone, in that moment, thought he was panicking, he took a deep breath and addressed the situation with a touch of humour. 'Well, technology does have a mind of its own sometimes.' This earned him a few chuckles, which lightened the tense atmosphere. Then, instead of apologizing for the messy situation, he used the opportunity to improvise. He reframed the disaster.

With his sharp wit and an engaging storyline, he launched into a free-flowing explanation of his presentation, holding the audience's attention with relatable anecdotes and passionate conviction. He even incorporated a mention of the glitch, turning it into a metaphor.

Sharma's authenticity and ability to think on his feet drew admiration from all quarters. His story serves as a testament to the power of reframing the disaster.

About Reframing the Disaster:

The best way to take control of a disaster is to reframe the view. How we view a disaster is one of the best ways to move ahead. Reframing a disaster is not positive thinking. Both are different methods. When we reframe a disaster, we do not change the events in any way.

To highlight what reframing the disaster is, I will give you an example. The sight from your window is wonderful but I draw the curtain. Now, when you look outside, the view appears blurred. I haven't changed anything outside. The sight is the same but now instead of being wonderful, it is hazy.

Instead of just rushing to find a solution to a problem, think of how to approach the disaster differently. Sometimes problems are not as big as we think they are. Humans tend to make a mountain out of a molehill. A slight shift in the way we see the problem can make a huge difference in solving it.

Reframing helps in generating more options and solutions. It is not about finding the real problem, but finding a better problem to solve. Be clear about the problem. What looks like disaster may be an opportunity. So what are we trying to solve here? Instead, we should be capitalizing on this as it is an opportunity. Get battered and shattered or be dynamic and dazzle. It all depends on what point of view you want to take.

When you apply this technique at the workplace, you will find that missing the project deadline had some meaning, not getting the promotion was better and getting laid off was perhaps the best thing to have happened to you.

Don't let a disaster be a disaster for you. Look for the blessing in it.

Action Points

Shift perspective:

1. Identify the silver lining—look for positives.
2. Focus on opportunities.
3. Concentrate on what you can control.

Practise gratitude and positive emotions:

1. Be grateful for what remains.
2. Look for light-hearted moments amidst the challenges.
3. Choose to maintain a positive outlook by focusing on rebuilding.

Seek support:

1. Identify potential allies or resources for specific challenge and establish initial contact.
2. Connect with others who share the experience.
3. Take professional help, if needed.

Remember,

Conquer or succumb.

62

Establish Credibility

To gain credibility, you must consistently demonstrate three things:
Initiative: You have to get up to go up. Sacrifice:
You have to give up to go up. Maturity:
You have to grow up to go up.

—John C. Maxwell

Megha often found herself overshadowed by her colleague, Ravindra. She was brilliant but low in confidence. Ravindra presented his ideas with confidence and that attracted attention and praise. Megha's ideas were always ignored because of her timid presentation.

Frustrated by this dynamic, she decided to do something about it. She approached her senior colleague, Ashok, for guidance. He told her that establishing credibility required not just presenting ideas but backing them up with knowledge, research and a genuine understanding of the needs and challenges at hand.

From then on, Megha was a new person. She actively participated in meetings, sharing her insights with confidence, because now she could back them up with solid research, evidence and thoughtful analysis. She began drawing attention and praise and her credibility started to build up.

By demonstrating her expertise, communicating effectively, delivering results and being authentic, Megha was able to inspire trust in others and establish her credibility.

About Establishing Credibility:

Credibility is the bedrock upon which leadership is built. It's earned through steadfast integrity and character. When your word is your bond, and your actions align with your values, trust becomes your currency. In the face of adversity, your steadfast principles illuminate your path and inspire those around you.

Your reputation is forged in the fires of initiative, sacrifice and emotional intelligence. Stay informed, be transparent and own your mistakes. Remember, credibility is a fragile asset, easily shattered but nearly impossible to rebuild. As Michael Josephson wisely said, 'Say what you mean and do what you say.'

Prioritize credibility over popularity. It's the compass that guides you through the complexities of leadership. Admirable leaders are those whose integrity shines brighter than any fleeting trend. They inspire not by force, but by the unwavering trust they inspire.

Action Points

Take initiative and solve problems:

1. Don't wait to be told what to do.
2. Be proactive by identifying issues and finding fixes for them.
3. Demonstrate honesty and integrity in everything that you do.

Communicate effectively:

1. Express your ideas and thoughts clearly and precisely.
2. Display sensitivity; know when to speak and when to keep quiet.
3. Be transparent.

Be reliable and dependable:

1. Don't miss deadlines.
2. Follow through on commitments.
3. Don't exaggerate and over-promise.

Remember,

By establishing credibility, you enhance your ability to persuade, inspire and drive change.

63

Be the Only One

If everybody is doing it one way, there's a good chance you can find your niche by going exactly in the opposite direction.

—Sam Walton

Dina worked as a junior accountant in MetroCorp. She was good at her work but was no more than a cog in a well-oiled machine. Her company was expanding fast, and she knew that if she didn't do something different to make herself valuable, she would be overlooked for promotions and would become just one among the crowd.

She noticed that China could be a potential market for MetroCorp, so she registered herself to learn Mandarin, a language unknown to anyone else in the company. After becoming fluent in it, she wondered if this new skill that she had acquired would really turn out to be an asset for her.

Her plan to *be the only one* in the company proved right in the coming days. A Chinese conglomerate sent a cryptic email laden with cultural nuances and subtle references that left seasoned executives scratching their heads. She was contacted and, after spending a few minutes deciphering the message, she realized it was a proposal for a joint venture, cloaked in cultural idioms.

In a meeting, she translated the proposal to senior management. The client was stunned with her fluency and the management team realized that she was invaluable because of her ability to become the bridge between cultures. She was the key to unlocking similar such lucrative opportunities.

Clients from China, intrigued by her cultural understanding, requested her presence in meetings. Her knowledge of Mandarin became her calling card, propelling her from the back office to the boardroom. She climbed up the corporate ladder fast and began organizing workshops on Chinese business etiquette.

By being 'the only one', she gained power and recognition and benefited the company by creating opportunities for it. Her success is a reminder to all of us that the most valuable skills in the corporate world do not always lie in the mainstream.

About Being the Only One:

If you carve a niche for yourself, you create a secure position for yourself in the workplace. So either achieve something or create something that can make a difference to the company and you. Look deep inside, and you will find that you are brimming with potential. Reconnect with it and set it free. We are all blessed with amazing capabilities that can help us explore possibilities and take us on the path of phenomenal growth.

Dehumo Bickersteth in his article 'CARVE Your Niche. Your Life. Your Rules.' published on LinkedIn on 8 July 2022 says that CARVE stands for:

Capabilities

Activities

Results

Value

Evaluation

So, if you have the *capabilities* and are willing to take *action*, then you will be able to produce *results* that will increase your *value* and on *evaluation*, it will be known that you have *carved a niche for yourself*. You will have a unique position or a role that will help you stand apart from the rest.

Identify your area of focus or specialization, the one you are most passionate and keen about, then consistently work to excel in it. Or spot a useful area that no one else has spotted and make yourself brilliant in it. When you have successfully carved a niche for yourself, you get noticed by people who normally wouldn't have bothered to know you. Your name reaches the highest level and you become a subject of discussion among the members of the senior management.

You start getting special treatment. Your reputation as an expert gets built. Richard Templar in his book, *The Rules of Work*, says, 'If the other bosses think you are a good idea then your boss really has to go along with it.'

Be the only one but being the only one doesn't mean much unless you can make a difference to everyone.

Action Points

Develop a unique and valuable skill set:

1. Know your industry and identify a niche.
2. Gauge your work and strive to become an expert in your niche.
3. Constantly work on upgrading your skills.

Cultivate unmatched problem-solving skills:

1. Sharpen your critical thinking and analytical skills.

2. Don't settle for the status quo; be innovative.
3. Anticipate problems and challenges and be proactive in developing solutions.

Voice your ideas:

1. Expressing your opinion can help you to establish your voice in the company.
2. Use meetings as an opportunity to showcase your skill and knowledge.
3. Offer suggestions to juniors to hone their skills.

Remember,

Stand alone to stand out and soar.

64

Avoid Tunnel Vision

*Learn to see the big picture. Often times, we get tunnel
vision and lose sight of the big picture and what we're
really trying to accomplish.*

—Robert Cheeke

Eric Ulis is the guy who claimed to have identified D.B. Cooper.
Cooper had hijacked a plane in 1971 and then skydived out of
it with the ransom money. More than fifty years later, no one
really knows (except for Eric Ulis) about Cooper's whereabouts,
though there are several theories.

Ulis devoted years of his life and spent plenty of money
to prove to the world that he was right. A stewardess, who had
seen Cooper closely because she had served him, said that the
suspect wasn't the same person, but Ulis refused to accept it. He
was completely convinced about his tunnel vision.

People like Ulis do not stop to consider the possibility
that they may be wrong. Their tunnel vision convinces them
that they are right. Therefore, they go on wasting time, money,
energy and effort in that elusive quest, to prove to the world that
they are right.

About Avoiding Tunnel Vision:

Don't focus on a specific outcome and base your decision on information and evidence you gather from that outcome. There are always other ideas. There are always different ways of looking at the same thing. Tunnel vision is a self-imposed prison, blinding you to opportunities and shackling your creativity.

Don't let stubbornness be your anchor. Explore alternative approaches. Don't focus on one outcome or get attached to the result you are hoping for. Consider multiple possibilities. Tunnel vision can take you away from your company's goals. You miss the forest for the trees, the movie for the teaser, the big picture for the small picture.

There's a thin line dividing confidence from arrogance. When you say *I also can do this*, it is confidence. But when you say *Only I can do this*, it is arrogance. Find out if you are being confident or arrogant. If you persist with tunnel vision, it is arrogance. Ask yourself, 'What am I missing here?' That's the first step towards eliminating tunnel vision.

Expand your perspective. When you do that, you will slowly emerge out of the tunnel, because then your vision will see lights that you hadn't seen before.

Avoiding tunnel vision is a good way to create an impression in the workplace. Your co-workers will not only feel comfortable working with you but will be able to share their own perspectives and ideas which may help you to see other possible outcomes.

Action Points

Adopt a different perspective:

1. Don't see what you want to see.
2. Don't introspect too much.
3. Continually assess the situation.

Step back:

1. Review progress from a wider view.
2. A mental shift can help you see things differently.
3. Visualize a bigger picture.

Seek out new information:

1. New information can spark innovative ideas, so stay updated with current industry trends.
2. Cross-pollination of ideas can broaden your way of seeing things, so network with people from different departments and industries.
3. Experiment by taking calculated risks.

Remember,

You are wrong if you think you can never be wrong.

65

Look the Part

Good grooming and hygiene are essential. It's never too early to start being concerned about your appearance—first impressions are everything.

—Robert Parish

In the prestigious office of a multinational bank, Vincent Lobo felt like a mismatched button on a bespoke suit. He was super with numbers but his thrift store wardrobe clashed with the impeccably tailored attire of his colleagues. Despite his sharpness, he felt invisible, his ideas dismissed before they could be given a chance.

He felt hopelessly out of place. His situation was noticed by Thomas, a veteran investment banker, who looked every bit the role he played. He called Vincent to his office and said, 'Look, mate, you have potential in you, I know that, but you need to look the part.'

'How do I do that, sir?' asked Vincent.

'Dress strategically,' said Thomas. 'That'll elevate your presence.'

Thomas even suggested some shops from where he could get the ideal clothing and recommended a tailor who would stitch suits with the right fit. Vincent did as advised by the seasoned banker. He discovered clothes that reflected his personality while exuding professionalism. His confidence multiplied manifold. He felt more empowered.

As he started dressing with intention, he noticed a shift in his interactions. While, at first, he was unable to express himself and felt awkward in the presence of his well-dressed colleagues, now he radiated confidence. He had begun to *look the part*. He realized that looking the part was about presenting oneself with respect and consideration for the work environment.

By looking the part, he was able to find his own voice within the corporate world. It became a tool for self-expression.

Talent alone is not enough. You have to look the part too. When you can combine the two, you can make rapid progress.

About Looking the Part:

Image is everything. It is critical in the workplace for it readies you for the next level. Your image, your overall personality, builds a perception about you. Books are judged by their covers. People are judged by the clothes they wear. Everything in this world is about visuals. You can't escape or ignore this fact. The way you dress and carry yourself will create the opportunities that you are looking for.

The best way to know if you look the part is to see what people one level above you are wearing. That will give you an idea of how far you are from looking the part. One's appearance plays an important role whether people accept it or not. And first impressions are often the last impressions. You can cast a spell on those around you if you dress smartly. You don't have to be dressed in designer wear or make a fashion statement.

All you must do is to wear the right clothing with the right accessories. Your appearance is a powerful tool that can enhance your professional image. Dress to command attention and exude authority. A strong personal brand precedes you, shaping perceptions before a single word is spoken.

By looking the part, you are influencing others, including your seniors. Looking the part can get you that coveted position you were dreaming of. It can give your confidence a boost, making you look more in control and command. The professional who always looks in control and command is the one who is followed by others.

Action Points

Be aware of the dress code:

1. Pay attention to how others dress.
2. Maintain professional polish.
3. Follow proper grooming methods.

Dress for the role you aspire for:

1. If you are aspiring to be a manager or a senior executive, dress the way managers and senior executives do.
2. Be mindful of days when you are meeting clients.
3. Invest in key wardrobe staples.

Develop your personal style:

1. Express yourself through subtle touches.
2. Focus on fit and quality.
3. Exude confidence; it is the most important accessory.

Remember,

Elevate your image to elevate your impact.

66

Create the Right Conditions

A strong, successful man is not the victim of his environment.
He creates favourable conditions. His own inherent force and energy
compel things to turn out as he desires.

—Orison Swett Marden

In a dusty village in Malawi, one of Africa's poorest nations, Chima, a poor but smart farmer, refused to surrender to the circumstances that he and his fellow villagers were afflicted with. While others bemoaned their fate, Chima spent his days studying old weather maps and forgotten agricultural texts to find a way to fight the drought that had left the fields parched.

One night, hunched over a flickering lantern, he stumbled upon a forgotten technique—water harvesting. This ignited a spark within him. Instead of waiting for the sky to open up, he could create the conditions required for survival.

While others remained doubtful and fearful, Chima started collecting rainwater in any container he could find. From old buckets to discarded basins, he used everything. He then dug a small pit in his field, lined it with clay and connected it to a network of channels to collect rainwater run-off.

He was called naive and foolish; some even labelled him mad. But Chima—fuelled by unwavering determination to create the right conditions—persisted. He toiled tirelessly, his callused hands testament to his resolute spirit. Little by little, the pit was filled with water.

Chima planted seeds—carrots, onions, beans, anything that could withstand the harsh climate. While the townsfolk still scoffed at his actions, he remained buoyant. And then came the miracle. The seeds sprouted, green tendrils defying the barren landscape. A ray of hope shone for the people.

Encouraged by his example, others adopted his methods. Soon, the once barren fields were dotted with pockets of green. Chima's story is a reminder that creating the right conditions for yourself is the key to overcoming adversity.

Don't wait for miracles to happen but create miracles. Rather, be the miracle.

About Creating the Right Conditions:

Creating the right conditions is akin to cultivating a fertile garden; it requires careful preparation, nurturing and patience. By cultivating the right conditions, individuals and organizations can maximize their potential and increase the likelihood of achieving their goals.

So, stop feeling sorry for yourself or cursing your present situation. Be the force that brings about change. You cannot be sulking and moping and hoping to achieve success. You must be in charge of the situation at all times.

You shouldn't wait until that perfect moment to do what you want to do because there is no perfect moment. Get started right away. Bring about the change that you want to see. In a utopian situation, all can be happy. But the one who is brave and courageous makes difficult times look easy.

Doubt and fear can paralyse people. Drive them away. They have no place in your life if you are aiming for success. In the workplace, you will come across many occasions when there's a dead end, when you and your team are staring at failure, when you are clueless about the next step. It's during these situations that you must create the conditions that work in your favour.

You are not a product of your fears. Your mind may try to convince you that you are not brave or intelligent or smart. Conquer your mind.

The results that you are seeing now are due to the conditions that you created in the past. You are the architect of your own destiny. Your outcomes are a direct reflection of your environment. If results aren't as expected, it's time to redesign your surroundings. Create a reality that propels you forward.

Action Points

Define your ideal work environment:

1. Know the conditions in which you do your best work.
2. Cultivate your own state of flow.
3. Don't let setbacks ruffle you.

Develop skills that grant flexibility and independence:

1. Invest in learning high-demand skills.
2. Build a strong personal brand.
3. Create opportunities that meet your needs.

Cultivate self-discipline:

1. Separate your work life from your personal life.
2. Establish a consistent work routine.
3. Don't do anything that might disrupt the creation of your desired conditions.

Remember,

> Either let conditions control you or find
> ways to control the conditions.

67

Prioritize

*Things which matter most must never be
at the mercy of the things which matter least.*

—Goethe

I had a habit of passing by my team member's workstations, chatting with them, and observing how each of them worked. Once I found Noah juggling a constant barrage of emails, phone calls and branch requests. Each task was like a burning ember demanding immediate action. And Noah was tackling everything simultaneously. I was alarmed by his working style because despite being busy, he didn't seem to be doing justice to his work. He looked hopelessly out of control.

I told him to meet me in my office before going home in the evening. I explained to him the importance of prioritizing. I suggested that he categorize tasks based on urgency and importance and free up time for critical tasks. I requested him to keep me posted about the progress he was making.

Initially, he found it challenging, as he was used to a particular way of working. But with practice and my encouragement, he would begin his day by outlining priority tasks, scheduling times for each and focusing solely on one at a time.

After a week or so, calm replaced chaos and Noah looked more assured and in control of the situation. His confidence soared and his productivity and quality improved.

About Prioritizing:

Your goals and aspirations will remain unfulfilled if you do not learn to prioritize. Blindly doing things without understanding their importance and urgency will take you further and further away from your dreams, leaving you unfulfilled, resentful and sad.

In the workplace, there is plenty of action, lots of instructions and tasks being assigned. You shouldn't allow yourself to get lost in this maze of confusion. Know how to prioritize your values.

What matters most should be tackled first. What is of least importance should be tackled after all important matters are completed. What is it that needs to be done right away? Focus on that.

How you prioritize work says a lot about you as a professional. Your ability to prioritize makes you an effective time manager, and time management is a key skill to have. You will be better equipped to make decisions and judgements.

Prioritization is your superpower. It turbocharges productivity, conquers chaos and calms the mind. Master this skill, and watch your performance soar.

To create an impact in the workplace, become a manager of priorities.

Action Points

Focus on high-impact tasks:

1. Maximize your impact by tackling the most important and urgent tasks.
2. Stick to the schedule.
3. Do not multitask. Focus on one task at a time.

Accomplish more in less time:

1. Align tasks with overall goals.
2. Don't shift your focus from priorities.
3. Make informed decisions.

Avoid procrastination:

1. Get going right away.
2. Identify tasks that can be delegated and eliminated.
3. Do not switch from one task to another until you have completed the one that you were doing.

Remember,

Without priorities, you're chasing shadows.

68

Build a Challenge Network

*What you need is a challenge network. I think of a challenge
network as the group of your most thoughtful critics who are able
to hold up a mirror so that you can see your blind spots and then
know what you need to rethink.*

—Adam Grant

When I was working with a regional bank in the Middle East,
I knew someone called Tony Peters, who was a CTO in an IT
company. He told me a story about Rujuta Thakkar, a passionate
young programmer in his team. We were attending an event
where the term 'challenge network' was used by one of the
speakers and I asked Tony about it and in response he told me
this story.

He said, 'Rujuta felt her creativity being stifled by
monotonous tasks and uninspiring deadlines. She was seeking
fresh perspectives, but her colleagues were too preoccupied with
their own work to offer them. So, one day, she gathered courage
and sent emails to several co-workers in different departments
who were facing the same challenges as she was.

'She received several enthusiastic responses. They decided to meet for weekly lunches. Soon this group became so engaged that everyone in the company came to know about it. The whole purpose of this group was to challenge each other on their knowledge, learning and ideas. Tough feedback was given, without any sugarcoating.'

'So, you get it,' Tony said, 'A challenge network is the antithesis of a support network. Whereas in a support network, you get plenty of encouragement and kind and inspiring words to lift you up, in a challenge network you get to hear the hard facts, sometimes in a harsh way. There's no beating around the bush; no one is there to please you. Your ideas are torn apart, your beliefs about a specific thing are challenged, your views are questioned . . . while a support network is all about cheerleaders, a challenge network is all about critics. Rujuta, from this one single action, was able to develop herself so fast that within a short period she rose up the corporate ladder, and I was pleased to recommend her promotion.'

About Building a Challenge Network:

How many people do we have in our lives whose criticism we value? Probably not more than two or three. And how many of us know people who will not let us settle down unless they are able to extract the best from us? People who will keep pushing us till we deliver the best outcome. Probably, none.

The presence of such people in our lives is essential for our growth and progress. Adam Grant, Wharton management professor—who coined the term challenge network—in his book *Think Again* explains why building a challenge network is an important ingredient for success. People who disagree with us, identify our blind spots, question us and do not hesitate to tell us what we lack are helping us to overcome our weaknesses.

Encourage your co-workers (if you can, form a team of five or six people) to challenge your assumptions. Let them argue with you, be ready to hear some disparaging remarks, give them the freedom to tear your ideas apart. This strategy will help you to get stronger and more assured of yourself. Without a challenge network, we might stray, become complacent and start thinking that we are perfect.

We all have biases. We all get overwhelmed with our thoughts. We think our understanding, our perspectives and our way of looking at things are faultless. But that could prove fatal. The challenge network will confront us to think and question and push us to the limit. In the end, when we make a decision, we will know that we took every possible step that we could to do our best. When we decide without the challenge network's involvement, you may have to face a nightmarish situation if your decision backfires. But when you decide with its involvement, you face a tough situation before making a decision. Lone wolf decisions risk catastrophic consequences. Involving a challenge network might be uncomfortable upfront, but it's a small price to pay for avoiding potential disaster.

If we are going in the wrong direction, the challenge network can point us in the right direction or convince us to start all over again.

Action Points

Define your challenge and target audience:

1. Be clear about the specific challenge your network will address.
2. Identify one key player who you trust.
3. Insist on brutally honest feedback—let them tear you apart.

Structure your network for accountability and support:

1. Create engaging platforms and activities.
2. Decide on preferred communication methods.
3. Be accountable to that one key player you trust.

Be committed:

1. Actively engage with challenge network members and commit to implementing at least one challenging suggestion or perspective into your work or personal life within a specified timeframe.
2. If you want to learn, improve and develop, do not give up.
3. Based on feedback received, implement the changes in your ideas, thoughts and personality, and keep evolving.

Remember,

Challenges are the crucible in which character is forged.

69

Love What You Do

The only way to do great work is to love what you do.
—Steve Jobs

We had a general manager who was known for his keen observation. He would often pass by our office, smiling and waving, while his eyes absorbed everything that was going on. Once, after his visit, I received a call from his secretary. 'Sir wants to see you,' she said. Before I could ask anything more, she had disconnected.

I was surprised by this spontaneous meeting. Usually our meetings were scheduled and I knew the agenda. But this time, I was clueless. I went to his office, my mind busy thinking. I was a bit nervous because I like to be prepared for meetings.

When I entered his office, he smiled at me and said, 'Sit, don't be so worried.'

I sat down. His eyes were fixed on me. 'Nasir Zaidi,' he said. 'You don't look happy. What's the matter?'

I silently saluted him. This man was a genius, I thought. I really wasn't happy. And the reason was my work. Doing the same stuff everyday was testing my patience. The day he had spotted me, I wasn't looking my normal self.

When I didn't answer his question, he said, 'Do what you love, and you will never work another day in your life.'

What he said touched my soul.

'Either quit and get involved with what you are passionate about or become passionate about what you are doing. That's all I want to tell you. You may go now.'

This meeting changed my perspective about the way I worked. I put my heart, mind and soul into my work, and from that day onwards, I never felt unhappy, stressed or bored.

The key is to love what you are doing or start doing what you love.

About Loving What You Do:

If you are doing something for the sake of doing it, you will always be dissatisfied, frustrated and angry. If you are constantly in such a mood, you will never be able to inspire yourself, let alone inspire anyone else at the workplace.

You spend so much time in office and if you don't love your job, it's like going to jail every day. A time will come when you will be facing a breakdown. This can lead to a breakdown.

The importance of loving what you do cannot be emphasized enough. When you love your work, you are motivated, inspired and high in spirits, and people around you will benefit seeing your enthusiasm and energy.

Loving what you do is a productivity booster and performance enhancer. Not only this, you will be more optimistic, more eager to learn and keener to share your learning. Your co-workers will be influenced by you and may also start loving their jobs. Whatever comes your way, you will tackle it with positivity.

Difficulties, delays, disturbances, disruptions, debates, disagreements, disappointments—you will be able to handle all this with a smiling face because of the passion that you have for your work. The thought of giving up on something will never cross your mind. Your passion will drive you and make you persistent.

Dislike doesn't dictate destiny. It's possible to transform aversion into affection. Cultivate a passion for what you once repelled, and watch your involvement deepen.

Great achievements are possible when you are passionate about your work. Nothing can stop your progress if you enjoy what you are doing. So, make a point to fall in love with your work or find work that you love.

Action Points

Align your passions with your purpose:

1. Find out what you don't like about your work.
2. Try doing that part of the work differently.
3. Be creative.

Challenge yourself:

1. Explore different aspects of your field.
2. Stagnation breeds boredom, so learn new skills.
3. Take on difficult assignments.

Cultivate a positive work environment:

1. Build strong relationships with colleagues.
2. Maintain a healthy work–life balance.
3. Infuse your work with a playful spirit.

Remember,

If you don't love what you do,
then every day will feel like a prison.

70

Work Smart, Not Hard

The most successful men work smart, not hard.
—Bangambiki Habyarimana

Yaqoob, a junior architect, was always buried under a mountain of work. His desk overflowed with blueprints, concept drawings, client's contracts and proposals. Despite his speed, his work never seemed to get over, and at the end of every day, he was exhausted and so overwhelmed that he felt like quitting.

His co-worker Bilal seemingly zipped through his tasks and always looked fresh and agile. One evening, as they were leaving the office, Yaqoob asked Bilal, 'How come you are so efficient, while I am drowning in work, when we have the same responsibilities and tasks?'

Bilal smiled. He said, 'It's about working *smart*, not *hard*. You work hard, I work smart.'

'How do you do that?' Yaqoob asked. 'Please share your ideas with me so that I too can become efficient by working smart.'

'You have to understand which tasks to tackle first, so make a priority list, then focus on the most important ones that need immediate attention and utilize tools, wherever you can, to save time.'

Yaqoob implemented the ideas. He started the day by listing and prioritizing tasks, focusing on the critical ones first, and utilized online project management tools to keep track of deadlines and other related tasks. He was now able to complete his work with more clarity and confidence and could also find time for creative exploration.

Rediscover the joy of working by being a smart worker, like Yaqoob did.

About Working Smart, Not Hard:

When you spend a considerable amount of time completing many things, that's hard work. Smart work is when you spend less time on completing the right things.

Spending more time doing many things is hard work. Spending less time doing the right things is smart work.

From hard work, we gain experience, while smart work comes from experience. While working hard, we are just performing a task. While working smart, we are doing the job in an efficient way. Hard work requires a lot of dedication, but the results are not visible. In smart work, even with tiny inputs, results are visible.

Hard work is toiling alone. It leaves one mentally and physically exhausted. Smart work is teamwork. It is productive and less taxing. When you work hard, you get frustrated and irritated. Such feelings don't arise when we work smartly.

In the workplace, those who work smartly will always be in greater demand, than those who work hard. This is because smart workers are more skilful. They select the right opportunities and have a clear picture of what they want to do and where they are going. They also know when and how to say no, which hard workers are unable to do.

Smart workers are not focused on tasks that they should do but are more inclined towards tasks that have the potential to create the biggest long-term impact. Most importantly, smart workers are more in control of their time and the situation.

So be smart, work smartly.

Action Points

Become tech-savvy:

1. Utilize technological tools like project management to-do listing or time-tracking apps like Clockify.
2. Once you have the right apps to fit your work style, bring them together through automation.
3. Measure your results, not your time.

Become organized:

1. Plan ahead.
2. Complete tasks in chunks.
3. Identify repetitive tasks.

Set up your workspace for success:

1. Think about how your workspace can aid in your workflow.
2. Declutter your desk.
3. Keep only those things that will facilitate your work.

Remember,

   If you strategize more, you will sweat less.

71

Be Interesting and Interested

To be interesting, be interested.
—Dale Carnegie

I have often come across people who talk too much and think that they are the life of the party. Like one of the managers in a bank I used to work in. His name was Stanley D'Souza. He was exceptionally boring because he talked too much and only about himself. In that same bank, there was another manager by the name of Pankaj Singh, who everyone found interesting because he always showed an interest in others.

His genuineness in knowing people, asking questions beyond small talk, made him popular. As he was interesting, he was able to attract people and by being interested in them, he was able to establish solid connections. Whenever he was in a meeting or a gathering or a party or even in a one-to-one discussion, it was always less about him and more about others.

He was an interesting storyteller and an interested listener, which made him likeable and lovable. That's why no one ever refused his requests. Everyone wanted him on their team whenever a project was assigned to them.

About Being Interesting and Interested:

No one likes boring people. We like to be with interesting people because they are fun to be around. Beauty, strength, intelligence—they all matter a lot, but it's also important to be an interesting person to talk to.

Interesting minds are idea factories, transforming workdays into playgrounds. Be the catalyst for creativity, the architect of engaging conversations. Your thoughts, words and perspectives are your unique paintbrush; create a masterpiece.

Genuine interest is magnetic. People gravitate towards those who truly listen, appreciate and uplift them. Become a master of connection by valuing others' perspectives and making them feel special. Your impact will grow.

Being interested means you are willing to strengthen the relationship, deepen it and make it more meaningful. At the workplace, it helps if you have meaningful connections with your co-workers because that makes working together less challenging and more exciting. Complex projects, pressing assignments, overload of work, all this can be tackled easily, because of the connection you have built by showing your interest in others. When you express your delight in others, they shine like the sun, and their radiance falls on you, making you glow too.

Being interesting can open doors for you that you thought could never be opened. You can connect instantly with people. And what is life if not connecting with others? Your perspectives are not outdated; they are fresh and new, and you are at your authentic best. All this combined makes you special.

Action Points

Become a storyteller and share experiences:

1. Weave experiences and information into interesting stories.
2. Don't just recount events; share the insights you have gained.
3. Speak with passion and enthusiasm.

Be a continuous learner:

1. Keep experimenting.
2. Learn new facts.
3. Read widely and explore new topics/subjects.

Show your interest in others:

1. Pay close attention to what others are saying.
2. Be generous with your compliments.
3. Focus on uncovering their perspectives, experiences and passions.

Remember,

Your capacity to fascinate others is directly correlated to your own engagement with the world; the more interested you are, the more interesting you become.

72

See All Points of View

*It is a narrow mind which cannot look at a subject
from various points of view.*

—George Eliot

Let me share the story of Nitin Paranjpe, a firebrand loan officer,
who worked with me in a bank in Mumbai. He was known for
his focus and ruthless efficiency. His aggressive tactics secured
quick loan approvals, boosting his individual performance.
His colleagues though disapproved of his methods. The main
fear was that he was overlooking crucial details while chasing
quick wins.

Yet, he was able to continue because no one questioned
him or made him see other points of view. Things changed when
Ashok took over as the risk manager. The first loan proposal
that Nitin sent him was for a promising start-up. Everything
was perfect, especially the impressive numbers, but Ashok had
his reservations. He highlighted potential risks in the financial
projections and recommended a more thorough investigation.

Nitin wasn't too happy about it. He scoffed at Ashok's
cautious approach and dismissed his reservations as unnecessary

delays. This conflict between the two presented a stark picture. The sales team always preferred quick deals over thorough risk assessments. They had their own reasons for doing so. They were driven by targets and commissions. This clashed with the risk management team's focus on safeguarding the bank's financial health.

Varsha Desai was Ashok's deputy. She observed the strained relationship between the two teams and took the initiative of bridging the gap. She engaged Ashok in a conversation, not about his reservations about the loan, but about his passion for risk analysis. She said, 'It's fascinating the way you can predict potential problems and safeguard the bank's future.'

Ashok explained to her the philosophy behind his actions and shared case studies of seemingly promising ventures that turned into financial disasters due to hidden risks. Armed with facts, she approached Nitin and gently described the rationale behind Ashok's concerns. She emphasized the importance of balancing tough targets with responsible risk management. This made Nitin think differently. Varsha had convinced him to see things not only from his angle, but from another's perspective too.

He agreed to take another look at the proposal based on Ashok's recommendation and henceforth, the two teams collaborated well together.

About Seeing All Points of View:

If you think you know everything, if you think only you are right and your point of view is the best, you are sadly mistaken. In effect, you have restricted yourself. You have become a hurdle in your own path to progress. So, the sooner you stop doing this, the better for you personally as well as professionally.

Learn to see things from every angle. Listen to the viewpoints of others. Do not make decisions without studying the matter from as many perspectives as possible. The right way is vital. That will make you realize that there are many more solutions to a problem than what you had thought of. Therefore, perspectives matter.

Do you remember that famous riddle? Acting on an anonymous phone call, the police decide to raid a house to arrest a suspected murderer. They don't know what he looks like but they know that his name is John. Inside the house they find a carpenter, a lorry driver, a car mechanic and a fireman. Without even asking him his name, the police nab the fireman. Why?

Many of us will be bamboozled and won't be able to find a solution to this. It is because of the way we see things. Our mind is already made up that all four people are men. We don't realize that women could be carpenters, lorry drivers and car mechanics.

When we convince ourselves to see all points of view, understanding and tolerance increases and things that once appeared big may begin to look small. We are very quick to come to conclusions, form opinions and pass judgements. It is always good to pause, reflect and ruminate, explore all angles and then decide.

The ability to take a 360 degree view can make you stand out in the workplace.

Action Points

Seek diverse inputs:

1. Consider the devil's advocate approach—assign someone to challenge assumptions and uncover potential blind spots.

2. Solicit feedback from multiple sources.
3. Find common ground with others.

Coach yourself to see things from different angles:

1. Practise seeing from different perspectives.
2. Use your imagination to consider a situation from a multitude of viewpoints.
3. Watch movies/TV shows/read books that highlight the importance of different perceptions.

Communicate openly and transparently:

1. Acknowledge the importance of dissent and constructive criticism.
2. Encourage questions and clarifications.
3. Provide a dedicated space for exploring varied views.

Remember,

Expanded perspective unlocks hidden truths.

73

Keep on Learning

If you are not willing to learn, no one can help you.
If you are determined to learn, no one can stop you.

—Zig Ziglar

Joy was a joy to have in my team. I thoroughly enjoyed collaborating with him during his three years he was with us. He was a continuous learner and his thirst for learning inspired me to become a lifelong learner.

He was not content with his performance and wanted to know how he could excel. That too wasn't enough for him. He wanted to know the why behind what he was doing wrong and he was not afraid to ask questions. Many co-workers scoffed, laughed and even ridiculed him for his queries and inquiries. But Joy wasn't bothered. His aim was clear. And that was to keep learning.

While many employees do not even know what the colleague sitting next to them is doing, Joy not only knew what his team members were doing, he also knew what co-workers in other departments were doing. He talked to everyone and discussed their work and exchanged ideas. He not only completed all the mandatory online courses that HR had initiated but also all the optional ones.

He attended all the training workshops that were relevant to his work and requested me to recommend him even for workshops that were not related to his work. He read a lot. He always carried a book. During lunch break, I often saw him catch up with his reading.

He went with employees—designated for testing new systems—to test and observe and asked questions to get his doubts clarified. He never hesitated to share his learning. He freely shared his knowledge and coached and mentored the juniors. He would tell me, 'Nasir sir, knowledge shared is knowledge gained.'

He sat with his peers and learnt from their experiences; he fixed meetings with seniors from various departments and absorbed their knowledge, becoming a mentor to a few, and actively sought mentorship from professionals inside and outside the organization.

This habit of continuous learning rapidly took Joy up the corporate ladder.

About Keeping on Learning:

If you don't keep learning, you will stagnate. But if you keep learning, you will know about new trends in your industry and improve your skills in key areas. Learn, unlearn, relearn, keep learning, that's the only way to move forward and remain ahead.

The hows and the whys differentiate the worker from the boss. The worker knows how, the boss knows why. Continuous learning will take you from the realm of how to the domain of why. If you keep learning, you will gain new perspectives, and new ideas will blossom in your mind.

Deloitte's continuous leaning model talks about three types of learning: Immediate, Intermediate and Transitional. To be successful in today's world, you will have to go for Immediate learning. But if you are looking to expand your current skills and grow from your current position, Intermediate learning will help you. For long-term organizational goals or for climbing up the corporate ladder or making a career switch, opt for Transitional learning.

Growth or safety, this is a call you have to take. If you choose safety, you needn't keep abreast of what's happening. Simply relax in your comfort zone. But if growth is what you are aiming for, seek discomfort. Through continuous learning, you will be able to develop yourself.

Continuous learning can be beneficial in several ways. Some of them are:

- networking opportunities and cultivating relationships
- improvement in productivity
- upgrading of existing skills and acquiring new skills
- leadership development

A novice remains content with traditional learning. An expert is one who is a continuous learner.

Action Points

Practise active learning:

1. Don't just passively consume information.
2. Engage in active learning techniques.
3. Move beyond simply repeating tasks.

Explore unfamiliar territory:

1. Tackle a problem outside your job description.
2. Meet with leaders of your company.
3. Learn from different sources—explore documentaries, blogs, online lectures and even museums or art exhibitions—to make learning more engaging.

Apply your learning:

1. Don't let your learning gather dust.
2. Apply your newly acquired knowledge and skills to real-world work scenarios.
3. Become a knowledge sharer.

Remember,

Stagnant water breeds decay; a closed mind breeds ignorance.

74

Forgive

The weak can never forgive. Forgiveness
is the attribute of the strong.

—M.K. Gandhi

After becoming President of South Africa, Nelson Mandela visited Robben Island, the prison where he was incarcerated for twenty-seven years during the apartheid. He met some of his former jailers, including the one who had treated him the harshest.

Mandela surprised one and all by requesting a meeting with this guard, the one who used to harass him by urinating on him. He greeted the guard warmly, and invited him to share a meal and conversation. The guard was scared, trembling, and expected Mandela to retaliate in a more brutal manner, either by torturing him or imprisoning him, as he was now the President.

But Mandela did neither. He said holding onto anger would only imprison him further. He believed that forgiveness was essential for his own freedom and well-being, as this would allow him to move past bitterness and build a better future.

Mandela's magnanimous gesture is a lesson for all of us. By forgiving, we can move ahead.

About Forgiving:

Whether at the workplace or outside it, forgiveness is not given the importance that it deserves. Perhaps, in their personal lives, you may see some people following this practice, but in office, one tends to remain adamant. If an argument or a misunderstanding takes place with a colleague, we just cut off relations with that person. We go to the office every day and we see that colleague with whom we have broken off ties and we make no effort to make amends.

We do not realize how this behaviour adds to our stress. By not forgiving, we are feeding the fire in us and that fire just keeps growing, consuming us from within. The longer we stay in a state of non-forgiveness, the more we suffer; this suffering affects our performance and productivity. Letting go is one of the best teachings of Buddha.

When we forgive, we offload the burden that our soul is carrying. We set ourselves free. We become light and our concentration and focus increases. Conflicts are bound to happen in the workplace because of pressure and competition. How we manage them shows our maturity as a professional. If some serious misunderstanding does occur and someone hurts us by words or deeds, getting upset is a normal reaction. If the person apologizes, forgive them immediately. And even if they don't, forgive them silently and get on with your work and life.

Practising forgiveness is a good way to develop stronger relationships and display team spirit.

Action Points

Understand the hurt, but don't justify the action:

1. Acknowledge the pain caused to you by the person who wronged you but don't try to justify their behaviour.
2. Focus on understanding the motivations behind their actions.
3. Fear, ignorance or their own pain may be the cause of their offensive behaviour.

Practise compassion:

1. Believe in giving the benefit of the doubt to others.
2. Actively challenge negative self-talk and replace it with self-compassionate statements.
3. Develop a forgiveness mindset.

Focus on 'letting go':

1. Assume the best intentions.
2. Give the benefit of the doubt.
3. Holding on to anger and resentment is like drinking poison and expecting the other person to get sick.

Remember,

Forgiveness is a gift to yourself.

75

Share Knowledge

Sharing knowledge is not about giving people something,
or getting something from them. That is only valid for information
sharing. Sharing knowledge occurs when people are genuinely interested
in helping one another develop new capacities for action; it is about
creating learning processes.

—Peter Senge

In a certain company, an experienced and senior manager had to suddenly quit because of health reasons. No one else had the same knowledge and skills. The company realized that there would be a serious knowledge deficit in his area of work, viz., delinquency and bad debt management.

So, the company launched a project plan that would aim to capture the expertise of the outgoing senior manager. Over a period of three months, two 'knowledge harvesters' identified by the company collected all knowledge about the financial collection process from the manager and conducted numerous follow-up interviews after he had officially left the company.

After the 'knowledge harvesters' had recorded the outgoing manager's knowledge, a new, single source of information on the subject was created, which enabled anyone to learn how to manage delinquent accounts and respond to debt events such as bankruptcy and collection.

The senior manager was a Key Person Risk to the organization and therefore every organization should ensure that they have the mechanism to counter this risk. Knowledge sharing is the best way.

About Sharing Knowledge:

Knowledge sharing is essential because *knowledge shared is knowledge gained*. Organizations do well when they encourage knowledge sharing. They have efficiency gains and greater innovation capacity. No one loses when knowledge is shared. It's a perfect win-win situation for everyone from the employees to the organization.

Whether you are an expert or a novice, you know something that others don't. If everyone in the organization starts sharing their knowledge, imagine what the workplace would look like. A whole new learning process system would be set in motion.

Some may say, perhaps what I know is of zero value because I am not the person who can make something better out of it. To this, Stanley McChrystal, the former commander of US and international forces in Afghanistan, said, 'You find that information is only of value if you give it to people who have the ability to do something with it. So instead of knowledge is power, sharing is power.'

We may have several ideas, but we don't have the power to implement them and so we just let them remain dormant within us. What purpose is this going to serve? But if we share those ideas with our seniors, those ideas may be able to see the light of day, and the organization may benefit. No matter who gets the credit, your goal should be to help the organization reach its goal.

We all know that learning is the key to success. Learners are both students and teachers. Teach what you know, learn what you don't. New hires, future leaders or remote workers, they all need to learn. Share your unique experiences with them. Do not think that if you share what you know, someone will move ahead of you. That's regressive thinking. Be progressive. Share your knowledge.

Action Points

Identify your expertise and package it effectively:

1. Identify the knowledge you have that your team members would benefit from, and share it.
2. Choose the right platform.
3. Package your knowledge in such a way that it is accessible and engaging for your target audience.

Engage with online communities:

1. Join online communities related to your area of expertise.
2. Participate in discussions, answer questions and offer helpful advice.
3. Establish yourself as a thought leader and create opportunities to share your knowledge more broadly.

Make knowledge sharing interactive:

1. Go beyond a monologue.
2. Create a competition-free environment.
3. Encourage interaction, be open to feedback and different perspectives.

Remember,

Either be like a candle that lights up a room or
the sun that brightens the world.
Illuminate like the sun, not flicker like a flame.

76

Empathize

*If you talk to a man in a language he understands,
that goes to his head. If you talk to him in his language,
that goes to his heart.*

—Nelson Mandela

I am reminded of an incident that took place while I was handling a sales team in a bank in Mumbai. Sandeep, the rising star of the team, was known for his relentless drive and sharp wit. He consistently exceeded targets, always delivering outstanding numbers, but his pursuit of success often came at the expense of his colleagues. He frequently took credit for team projects and belittled those who fell short of his standards. He was respected for his skills but was considered cold and unapproachable.

One day, I asked him to prepare a pitch for a prominent client. The task wasn't easy, because a lot of complexities were involved. The client was high-profile, the product was new, and time was short. At first, he felt confident that he could do it, but as he delved deeper, and with the clock ticking, he realized that the assignment was way above his league.

After struggling and with his confidence faltering, he approached Neha, a seasoned member of my team. She was patient, had a collaborative spirit, and was like a guiding star. He had rubbed her the wrong way several times in the past. But she dealt with the situation with her usual calm manner. Sandeep knew that if there was anyone in the team who could help him to get this task done, it was Neha.

All she had to do when he came to her was to politely refuse to assist by cooking up an excuse, but to his utter surprise, she did not do so, nor did she mock him for seeking help. She was accommodating and listened attentively as he expressed his worries. She even acknowledged his achievements while gently pointing out how his actions might be impacting others. She brainstormed with him and guided and supported him till he was able to prepare the pitch.

Neha's behaviour was an eye-opener for Sandeep. He understood the tremendous role that empathy played. He changed his working style and became more approachable and empathetic towards his co-workers.

About Empathizing:

Every individual has needs, thoughts and feelings. If we are unable to understand their needs, thoughts and feelings, we won't be able to connect with them. That would be a big miss, because without connecting with people, we can't do much.

In a research study, conducted by the Center for Creative Leadership, 'Managers who were rated as empathetic by their direct reports were also rated as high performing by their own boss.' Compassion connects. Once you establish that connection, work becomes productive because employees become supportive of each other.

In office, we are always in a hurry to finish our work, give our views, talk at length about our achievements, make presentations, attend meetings, give instructions and everything else that we do at the workplace. We forget that we are not alone. We have co-workers. All co-workers are not at the same level. But everyone has the need to feel wanted and be heard and understood. If we can give them the comfort of being wanted and let them know that they are understood, working relationships will be strengthened.

Dismissing others' experiences with platitudes erodes trust. True connection arises from understanding another's perspective, not dismissing their feelings. That acknowledgement, that acceptance of their emotions without passing judgement of any kind, is empathy.

Be genuinely interested in your team member's needs and goals to create deeper bonds. This will help in improving collaboration, because you will know each other's strengths, areas for improvement and working styles. Stress levels will decrease as conflicts will decrease, creating a more harmonious atmosphere, thus having a positive impact on the overall work culture.

So, empathize to rise.

Action Points

Give your full attention:

1. Put away distractions and concentrate fully on the person you are communicating with.
2. Understand a team member's problem from his/her point of view.
3. Listen beyond words.

Put yourself in their shoes:

1. Challenge your biases.
2. Imagine their situation; try to see the world from their point of view.
3. Avoid judging.

Respond with kindness and care:

1. Know the difference between sympathy and empathy.
2. Encourage, inspire, motivate.
3. Demonstrate small acts of kindness like sending a thoughtful message, offering to help with a task, holding the door open.

Remember,

Apathy builds walls, empathy builds bridges.

77

Give to Receive

The more you give, the more comes back to you, because God is
the greatest giver in the universe, and He won't let you outgive Him.
Go ahead and try. See what happens.

—Randy Alcorn

My senior colleague, Sunil Das, was an amazing guy. I was inspired by the way he conducted himself in office and learnt many things that I incorporated into my own life.

He always made himself available for his team. A thirty-minute slot was fixed permanently on his calendar for his team to see him, whenever he was in office.

He was ready to assist everyone in his team and even those from other departments. People reached out to him even from outside the organization. He always praised people, and highlighted their good qualities, contributions, knowledge and attitude.

I always found him to be proactive in supporting his manager. His intention was always to make things easy for his seniors and his juniors. What was surprising was that he went about doing all this without expecting anything in return.

I asked him, 'Why are you so giving?'

He answered, 'To receive, you should give first.'

That message has stayed with me.

About Giving to Receive:

When you give, you make space for new things to come to you. Giving could be anything. In the workplace, it could be your knowledge, time, constructive criticism, compliment, attention. Giving matters because by giving, you are expressing gratitude. By giving, you touch the hearts and souls of people.

Co-workers reciprocate favourably if you give first. But do not give with the intention of receiving. If that's the intention, you had better not give, because expectation always leads to frustration. Give with an open heart and then don't think about it.

If you see a colleague struggling with learning a skill, teach him how to do it. If another colleague wants to share her experience with you, give her your time. Maybe you are unhappy with a team member's performance, give them constructive criticism and help them to improve. If you are pleased with a team member's performance, praise them. Someone wants your attention, give it to him.

What you give, you will receive manifold. That's a universal law. So focus on giving whatever and whenever you can. By giving, you help others, you inspire more giving, you cultivate self-worth, you understand more about what responsibility is. You find a greater meaning to life, a purpose that can drive you to achieve much more. Don't wait to give things in large quantities. Start with smaller portions. Frequency matters, not the quantity.

Give and see how it benefits you.

Action Points

Shift your focus from transaction to contribution:

1. Focus on offering value first.
2. Think abundance, not scarcity.
3. Create a desire to contribute positively, not a sense of entitlement to receive something back.

Build relationships:

1. Set aside time for others.
2. Offer to help whenever you can.
3. Be liberal with compliments.

Give what you want to receive:

1. Reflect on the things you value most in your interactions with others.
2. Encourage reciprocity by embodying it yourself.
3. Create a giving circle.

Remember,

What you give comes back to you. So part with knowledge if you want to gain more knowledge. If you are looking for support, be supportive of others.

78

Turn Your 'I-Have-To' into 'I-Want-To'

Every day the clock resets. Your wins
don't matter. Your failures don't matter.
Don't stress on what was, fight for what could be.
—Sean Higgins

Vijay groaned, pulling himself from the warmth of his bed. The thought of the gym filled him with a familiar dread. 'Another workout,' he muttered, the words tasting like a bitter pill.

I asked about his morning routine. 'Woke up, but didn't go,' he confessed. 'Feels like punishment.'

'That's a problem,' I replied. 'When exercise becomes a chore, it's easy to resent it. You need to shift your perspective.'

'How?' Vijay asked, his brow furrowed.

'Instead of "I have to," try "I want to",' I suggested. 'It's about changing your mindset, seeing the gym as a place of growth, not a prison.'

Vijay considered this. 'I never thought of it that way.'

'Exactly,' I said. 'When you view exercise as a choice, not a compulsion, you'll find yourself looking forward to it. The benefits are countless.'

'Can I apply this to work too?' he wondered.

'Absolutely,' I replied. 'This mindset shift can transform any aspect of your life.'

About Turning Your 'I-Have-to' into 'I-Want-to':

The outcome of any action depends on your state of mind. It's all a mind game. If your thought is that you must do something, it shows that your heart is not in it.

You are doing that action out of compulsion, reluctantly. The outcome of anything done half-heartedly is half-hearted. It doesn't bring any cheer because you did the stuff despairingly. Unless you are enthusiastic, raring to go at a task, you won't get the desired result.

But when you choose to do something, it signifies a genuine passion and commitment to it.

To get the desired result, you must desire the action and take the steps required to get the work done. So, find the motive for doing a specific task. Maybe it is not worth it and you are doing it because you have been doing it or because your predecessor was doing it.

You shouldn't *just* do something. There must be a purpose. If you can't find it, don't do that work. Doing something without a purpose makes no sense.

'Have to' takes the power away from you. 'Want to' gives you control. When you shift your focus to why you want to do a task, and you get the answer/s then you would want to do it and when you want to do it, then you become a transformed person.

You become highly energetic and enthusiastic and you tackle the task with 100 per cent involvement. You become a different person. No obstacle can stop you because you will find ways to overcome it.

So, the sooner you change your 'have-to' into 'want-to', the better it is for you and your organization.

Action Points

Reframe the task and identify underlying values:

1. Understand your intentions.
2. Change the way you look at things.
3. Connect the tasks to your values (*I have to clean my workspace* becomes *I want to create a clean and organized workspace* (value: creating a clutter-free environment).

Increase your control and ownership:

1. Explore ways to approach the task with more autonomy.
2. Identify key areas where you can exert more control over tasks or projects to enhance motivation and productivity. Imagine completing the task successfully and experiencing the positive emotions associated with accomplishment.

Put yourself in discomfort:

1. Start with things that you don't feel motivated to do.
2. Reward yourself for progress.
3. Keep challenging yourself to do at least one task every day that you don't like.

Remember,

'Have to' is demotivating but 'Want to' is
a powerful motivator. 'Have to' makes you powerless,
'Want to' empowers you.

79

Learn to Accept

God grant me the serenity to accept the things I cannot change, the courage to change the things I can, and the wisdom to know the difference.
—Reinhold Niebuhr

'It's not good enough,' these words echoed and re-echoed in Elena's mind. Her novel had been declined by the publisher and she was unable to accept the rejection. Tears kept flowing from her eyes and she felt shattered. A week passed and she still felt the same. The words 'It's not good enough,' kept haunting her. She had poured her heart and soul into the story and was confident that her manuscript would be accepted. Badly affected by the rejection, she stopped writing and went deeper into depression.

Her father, a writer himself, sat down with her one day and said, 'Elena, writing is not for publishing. Writing is for joy, for pursuing your passion. Don't let rejection stop you from doing what you love doing. Accept the rejection. Then get going with your writing. Enjoy the journey and if on the way, you get published, well and good, otherwise keep writing for that will keep you happy and motivated.'

Her father's words had an amazing effect on her. *Accept the rejection*. These three words impacted her even more deeply. She told herself that the rejection had nothing to do with who she was, neither as a person nor as a writer. Once she was convinced that acceptance was the way forward, she was able to emerge out from her depression and focus on what she loved doing the most, writing.

About Learning to Accept:

Nothing is perfect. Even if you are occupying the corner office at work or have a fancy title and humungous salary, you will still have your share of worries.

The environment may not be as expected, some co-workers might be unbelievably irritating, the career path within the company may not be well defined, the coffee may be tasteless. There could be several irritating factors at the workplace. If you get overwhelmed by them, your energy will get dissipated and you will not be able to focus on your work.

So, learn to ignore what you can't control. Focus on what needs to be done. Learn to accept. You can't change people and situations because you have no control over them, but you can control your response. Therefore, instead of losing your cool, getting irritated or angry because you are in a resistance mode, just accept. Otherwise, the turbulence inside you will persist.

Acceptance releases you, sets you free. You become another person, a completely new you. You become happier, more relaxed and more peaceful.

To accept or not is a choice. The wise choose to accept. Acceptance fosters awareness, humility and contentment, creating a sense of inner balance. Once you have conquered the situation with acceptance, you become stronger and more focused, and you are able to discharge your duties in a professional manner.

Seeing you manage yourself in this way, your co-workers too will be inspired to change.

Action Points

Raise your self-awareness:

1. Remember *this too shall pass.*
2. Acknowledge the situation, however painful it may be for you.
3. Ask yourself 'Why can't I accept this?' Is it a belief that things should be a certain way, or a fear of loss of control?

Focus on what you can control:

1. Acknowledge the present moment.
2. Detach yourself from the outcomes—focus on your thoughts, actions and reactions.
3. Concentrate on what you have, instead of what you don't.

Look for opportunities:

1. Even the darkest clouds have a silver lining.
2. Ask yourself what I can learn from this?
3. Accept that life is not perfect; embrace imperfection.

Remember,

Acceptance is the liberation from the shackles
of misery and depression.

80

Own Your Mistakes

Acknowledge, that you failed, draw your lessons from it,
and use it to your advantage to make sure it never happens again.
—Michael Johnson

Shagufta's presentation was a disaster. She had painstakingly worked on it for weeks but at the appointed hour, she fumbled badly, and the technical glitches worsened the situation. Around her were confused looks and she had the urge to crawl under the table.

Back at her desk, she fumed and fretted. Finally, frustrated, she slammed her laptop shut and wept inconsolably. Her manager caught a glimpse of her crying while passing by her cubicle.

He stepped inside her cubicle and sat silently for some moments until Shagufta was able to compose herself. 'Look, Shagufta,' he said. 'Life is all about making mistakes. You need to make mistakes to grow.'

Shagufta listened to him wide-eyed, absorbing every word that her boss uttered. 'Just own your mistake and move on,' he said, and walked out of her cubicle. Taking a deep breath, she decided to do as her manager had advised. She emailed everyone present, acknowledging the technical issues and apologizing for the poor presentation. She even offered to reschedule and address any questions they might have.

She had not expected the response she got. Several colleagues replied with empathy, sharing their own similar experiences. Her manager called to tell her that she had done the right thing and offered support.

By owning her mistake, Shagufta didn't diminish her image, but had strengthened it, fostering trust.

About Owning Your Mistakes:

One quote that I like the most on 'mistakes' is from former US ambassador to Poland, Georgette Mosbacher. She says, 'Just because you make a mistake doesn't mean you are a mistake.' Making mistakes is evidence that you are working. Only those who don't do anything can avoid making mistakes.

I know that mistakes are taken very seriously in the workplace. But unless they are a result of gross negligence, mistakes shouldn't be used as a weapon against employees. The other thing that generally happens in the workplace is not admitting one's mistakes. That's unacceptable and unprofessional.

Hiding one's mistakes should be avoided. Taking ownership of your mistakes indicates a strong character and demonstrates a sense of responsibility. You are seen as a thorough professional. Owning your mistakes builds trust and enhances your credibility. It's a powerful tool of leadership.

Making a mistake is only human. Owning up is part of being a leader. It displays courage; it can prevent the bad from getting worse. It earns respect, turns the negatives into positives, helps you face your fears head-on and makes you look in command.

Professional relationships get strengthened because your manager considers you reliable, trustworthy and courageous. Of course, work in such a way that mistakes are avoided, but if they happen, there is no reason to panic or to cover it up; tell your boss about the mistake, learn your lessons and move on. Integrity is the cornerstone of a successful career, and owning your mistakes demonstrates integrity.

Committing the same mistakes repeatedly is a mistake. That should be avoided.

Action Points

Take responsibility and acknowledge the impact:

1. Do not look for excuses if you have made a mistake.
2. Express your regret for any inconvenience, frustration or harm caused.
3. Do not justify or make excuses.

Develop a solution-oriented mindset:

1. Have a solution plan ready.
2. Offer to fix the problem yourself (if possible).
3. Be open to feedback and guidance.

Demonstrate accountability through action:

1. If you offer solutions, be sure to follow through on your commitments.
2. Reflect on the lessons learned.
3. Show improved performance going forward.

Remember,

A leader's authenticity shines through
when they openly acknowledge their errors.

81

Recharge

Rest is not a luxury; it is a necessity. Take the time
off to replenish your energy and recharge your soul.
In the midst of life's chaos, find solace in the stillness
of rest that is where true rejuvenation resides.

—Dr Lucas D. Shallua

I recall Mayank Oza, one of the team leaders in my department, who worked like a maniac. He was a workaholic of the highest order. I never found him taking breaks or relaxing. Once, fully exhausted, both physically and mentally, he was not able to complete a task, which normally he would have finished in a matter of days. Staying back after hours, guzzling coffee and continuously working had drained his well of inspiration.

Seeing his condition, I had a chat with him. In the past too, I had pointed out that the way he was working, he was headed for a breakdown. But this time, I had a detailed discussion with him.

'Your dwindling energy and declining work quality is because of your working style and if you don't change it, you will burn out,' I said. 'Taking a break isn't a failure. Getting yourself recharged is essential.'

I allowed him a two-day break which he reluctantly agreed to take. When he came back, he was a different Mayank. His mind was clear, his energy renewed. With a fresh perspective and bubbling with enthusiasm, he tackled the task he had been struggling with, and within a couple of days, he was able to complete it with impeccable quality.

Prioritize your well-being by getting yourself recharged regularly.

About Recharging:

Even if you are a workaholic, you need to take a break. Professional work is demanding, exhausting, tough and draining. If you just keep working without rebooting or recharging yourself, you will crack soon. That could prove dangerous for you as it may lead to long-term issues, with reference to your mental well-being.

Working continuously can affect productivity because your concentration will not be the same. Your pace of work will slow down. You will find it hard to motivate yourself, and you will struggle to manage. Chances are, you will make more mistakes.

Pushing yourself day in and day out can lead to burnout. Many employees experience this throughout the world. You must set aside time to rejuvenate. Recharging yourself is mandatory for your physical and mental health.

Don't get consumed by work. Remember that famous adage, *All work and no play makes Jack a dull boy*. Don't be like Jack. Or else your creativity will suffer, your thinking will not be as sharp, and you will have trouble motivating the team because you yourself will lack motivation.

It doesn't matter whether you have been working for a couple of years or a decade. Recharging is a must. Take small breaks throughout the day. A five-minute stroll or stretching or listening to your favourite music could just be what the doctor ordered. Any of these activities will infuse energy in you and you will be a different person.

I have seen employees working non-stop, not even getting up to go to the loo to relieve themselves. They miss lunch; they don't drink water throughout the day. They just keep working.

Withdraw from work because work will not withdraw from you. I used to carry a book with me to office and after every hour, I would read a few pages to refresh my mind. I would also walk around, stretch, take the stairs, call home and chat with co-workers. So, stay fresh by recharging yourself at regular intervals.

Action Points

Disconnect to reconnect:

1. Stretch.
2. Read something motivating (a poem, an article or a few quotations).
3. Talk to a family member or friend.

Engage in nature:

1. Go for a walk in the park.
2. Watch the sunrise and sunset.
3. Listen to the birds sing.

Nourish your mind and body:

1. Dedicate time for activities you find fun and fulfilling.
2. Eat healthy foods and stay hydrated.
3. Prioritize quality sleep.

Remember,

> If you burn the candle at both ends,
> your brilliance will diminish rapidly.

82

Stick to Your Principles

In matters of style, swim with the current;
in matters of principle, stand like a rock.

—Thomas Jefferson

Everyone had left the office. Only Mujtaba Hussain, a talented young programmer, and his charismatic manager, Nawaz Bux, remained. They were in Hussain's brightly lit cubicle. Bux leaned over Hussain's desk, his smile widening, 'We have a tight deadline, Hussain. The code needs some . . . some adjustments to meet the client's expectations.'

A knot of anxiety tightened in Hussain's stomach. He knew what his manager meant. The 'adjustments' that he was talking about involved cutting corners on security protocols, something that he was vehemently opposed to. But his manager was pushing him to do exactly what he knew he shouldn't do. It was against his principles, and he wasn't going to compromise.

Bux placed his hand on Hussain's shoulder, his grip firm, and, in a voice dripping with false sincerity, said, 'It is okay to bend the rules sometimes. This is a moment for you to shine. Don't let go of the opportunity.'

Hussain recalled what his mentor would always say. 'Integrity and ethical conduct are non-negotiable.' Gathering courage, he looked Bux straight in the eye, and said, 'I cannot compromise on my principles, sir, but I am happy to work on alternative solutions even if it takes me the entire night.'

'So you won't do it,' Bux said.

'No, sir. I refuse to risk the security of our users.'

Bux's smile had transformed into a grimace by now. Casting an angry look at Hussain, he stormed off.

Hussain heaved a sigh of relief. He was still nervous but glad that he had stuck to his principles even in the face of pressure.

About Sticking to Your Principles:

What do you stand for? The answer to it defines your personality and who you are as a professional. If you don't stand for something, working with you will not only be difficult but also impossible. As Malcolm X said, 'A man who stands for nothing will fall for anything.' It shows that you have no values and someone who has no values has no value.

To create the right impact, stick to your principles. Never compromise on them. Maintaining a balance between steadfast principles and adaptability is essential. Values can be adjusted to fit new realities, but this should be a deliberate and rare occurrence.

In the workplace, you will face many situations that will test your principles. Stand like a rock, as Thomas Jefferson says. Do not budge. When it comes to integrity, there's no shortcut. There's no negotiation on this at all. It's like a *Lakshman rekha*. Excellence is another principle you should never compromise on.

Sacrificing your beliefs will make you hollow from inside. When you work with your principles intact, you can navigate through various obstacles, and produce quality work. Keep looking within and listening to your conscience that warns you when you are about to do something wrong.

Rising up the corporate ladder is what every ambitious professional desires to do, but if rising up means doing away with your principles, it's not worth it. A fake professional always falls.

Sticking to your principles enables you to be clear about your wants and helps you gain self-respect, while facilitating decision-making.

Action Points

Internalize your values and make them concrete:

1. Know what principles are non-negotiable in your life.
2. Connect values to actions.
3. Imagine positive outcomes associated with upholding your principles.

Develop coping mechanisms:

1. Identify triggers and temptations.
2. Equip yourself with phrases and mental tools to gracefully decline requests that conflict with your principles.
3. Have a supportive network of people equally conscious of sticking to values.

Stay focused:

1. Pursue excellence.
2. Know when to be accommodating (when your values are not getting compromised) and when not to (when your values are getting compromised).
3. No need to imitate or mimic anyone else.

Remember,

Compromising principles erodes one's identity.

83

You Can't Change Others

You can't change people but you can effect
a change in them by your behaviour.
                                    —Garrison Wynn

Horace, the hedgehog, shared a burrow with Fiona, the Fox. While Horace was orderly, Fiona was disorderly. Horace was constantly irritated with Fiona's messy habits. He tried everything he could to change her. He lectured her, rearranged her belongings, even constructed barriers in the burrow. But nothing worked.

Fiona, free-spirited and carefree, remained unfazed by Horace's attempts. Horace became frustrated. Exhausted, he retreated to a corner to reflect. He recalled his grandma's words, 'Sometimes, the only thing you can change is your perspective.' He decided to let Fiona be as she was. Instead, he started focusing on his own reactions and responses.

He started ignoring the clutter and concentrated on his own space and activities. He subtly incorporated playful games and puzzles into his routines, arousing Fiona's curiosity and encouraging her to be more mindful of her surroundings.

While Fiona was still disorganized, she became more conscious of her habits. They coexisted peacefully thereafter.

Acceptance and adaptation are more effective than attempting to change the unchangeable.

About You Can't Change Others:

Most of us are desperate to change others. We want control over their thoughts, behaviours and choices. We don't realize that these things are beyond our control. Remember this and your life will change dramatically.

Every individual is unique. They have their own way of functioning, just like you and I do. We too are different from others and have our own special way of operating.

No one will behave the way you want them to behave. If you expect someone to talk in a particular way, or deal with you in a specific manner, it is not going to happen. Lower your expectations from other people, or better still, don't have any. Elevate your response when faced with subpar behavior.

Everyone has problems. Learn to live with that fact and move on. At work, your co-workers will behave the way they want to, and not the way you want them to, so do not get upset, irritated, frustrated or angry. Manage your emotions.

You are aggressive at work and so you want everyone to be aggressive like you. Or you take time to do stuff and so you expect the same kind of calmness from others; that's not the right attitude.

Change your approach. Change your ways. Change the way you think. You are the master of yourself. Keep adjusting and altering your work and communication styles. Let others be as they are and you be as you are and create synergy between yourselves.

Extend support, set an example, listen and empathize, encourage and motivate, do this with your colleagues and who knows, some may follow your lead. But even if they don't, you continue to drive the change within yourself.

Action Points

Focus on your sphere of influence:

1. Accept people for who they are.
2. Let it be or let it go.
3. Don't be demanding or commanding.

Practise acceptance and detachment:

1. Don't link your happiness or well-being with the behaviour of others.
2. Let go of the need to control the outcome of situations.
3. Observe situations and people without judgement.

Be yourself, be authentic:

1. Let your actions and behaviour reflect the change you wish to see in others.
2. Focus on creating and sharing positive examples to motivate and inspire desired behaviour, rather than solely relying on pressure tactics.
3. Invest your energy in self-growth.

Remember,

Concentrate on your own journey, not someone else's.

84

Keep Zero Expectations

*Blessed is he who expects nothing, for he
shall never be disappointed.*

—Alexander Pope

Yogitaa, my friend's daughter, landed a dream job at a prestigious news agency. Visions of groundbreaking investigative pieces and bylines on major stories danced in her head. She believed that within a short time, she would get the juiciest of assignments and her dreams would flower and flourish. However, reality was something else. She was assigned mundane tasks like fact-check and summarizing press releases, nothing related to the impactful journalism she craved.

Her initial enthusiasm began to wane. Disappointed, she began to dread work. She shared her frustration with her father, who requested me to talk to her. I knew how dreadful a feeling it was to work with unfulfilled expectations. I had seen many of my co-workers, both juniors and seniors, experiencing the same situation as Yogitaa, when I was working. I too had faced this. So, I told her what my mentor had told me.

'Yogitaa,' I said, 'Sometimes the most rewarding experiences come from having zero expectations. Approach

271

each task, no matter how insignificant, with an open mind and a dedication to do your best.'

'You mean, I shouldn't expect glamorous assignments to come my way,' she said.

'You shouldn't expect anything,' I said. 'Just treat each task as an opportunity to learn.'

She took my advice seriously and implemented it straightaway. She began going to the office without any expectations. Whatever work was given to her, she did it with thoroughness and attention to detail. She worked hard even on unimportant and insignificant tasks and actively sought feedback from her seniors.

Seeing her dedication and meticulousness towards fact-checking, her editor began assigning her small investigative tasks related to larger stories. This experience became a turning point for her. By keeping zero expectations, she was able to learn and enjoy her work and the kind of assignments that she had once craved began coming her way.

About Keeping Zero Expectations:

Expectations can easily turn into frustration. When frustration takes hold, it tends to give rise to aggression, hostility, anger and defensiveness. If these emotions aren't handled well, they can snowball into stress. In a work environment, this frustration often leads to mistakes, lower efficiency, a lack of energy and missed deadlines. Isn't that setting the stage for disaster?

Creating a zero-expectations mindset can do wonders for you. You won't get frustrated because your expectations from your colleagues, seniors, HR and management will be nil. Your focus will be only on work. You can then give your best, but expect nothing. If you work, keeping expectations in mind, it will mar the experience. Your mind will focus on the outcome, thus affecting your working style and process. This will lead to a dip in quality.

Creating a zero-expectations mindset is not easy but then what is? You must put in effort for everything. But once you develop that mindset, it is both liberating and challenging. Liberating because you will be working without any specific result in mind and challenging because progress will be difficult to measure as there are no clear expectations.

Practising mindfulness, being self-aware and having a flexible outlook can help you to develop a zero-expectation mindset. With this mindset, you will be a force to reckon with at the workplace and in total control of yourself and the situation.

Action Points

You are the key:

1. To be at peace with yourself, give up your expectations.
2. Do good, not with the intention that good may be done to you.
3. Rely only on yourself.

Appreciate what you have:

1. Don't bother about what you don't have.
2. Practise gratitude.
3. Find joy in the little things.

Practise non-attachment:

1. Desire things and work to obtain them, but detach your happiness from the fulfilment of those desires.
2. Don't get attached to what you have.
3. Be open to unexpected joys and possibilities.

Remember,

Without expectations, every experience is a fresh start.

85

Do Not Criticize Others

*Any amount of time you spend criticizing others is time you
could spend improving yourself.*

—Nate Miller

Humphrey, the Hippopotamus, was known for making a
mess of everything. Peter, the Peacock, always criticized him
for his sloppiness. Once, in the morning, when Humphrey
lumbered past, his mud-caked hooves leaving a trail of dirt
and grime, Peter said in disgust, 'Have you no shame? Look at
the state of you!'

Poor Humphrey, already embarrassed, hung his head
lower and, mumbling an apology, hurried away, feeling worse
about himself. Oliver, the Owl, hooted from his branch, 'Peter,
do not criticize others. Look at your own feet. Aren't they ugly,
while your plumage is so beautiful?'

Peter was stunned by Oliver's remark. He looked down at
his feet and then turned to look at his plumage. Oliver saw him
doing that. 'Now if everyone focused on your feet, instead of
your plumage, how would you feel?'

'You are right, Oliver,' said Peter. 'But how should I deal with Humphrey?'

'Criticism without compassion pricks, just remember that. When you next see him, offer him a solution instead or else, say nothing.'

Peter changed his approach completely and stopped criticizing Humphrey. 'Maybe you can take a bath before you come this side,' was all that he said. Surprised by his kind suggestion, Humphrey started doing that.

Offer solutions instead of criticism to foster a more harmonious environment.

About Not Criticizing Others:

Criticism doesn't change an individual's behaviour. It only makes them more rigid and defensive, and of course, angrier. So, criticism can never work as a motivating tool. It causes relationships to sour and makes it hard for people to work together.

Even when someone asks you for criticism, as per W. Somerset Maugham, they are in fact asking for praise. So, do not get carried away. Maintaining healthy relationships is essential, because you never know whose support you may require. If the relationship is broken, it becomes awkward and embarrassing to work together or to seek help and opinion.

Yes, disagreements will happen, but don't let them go out of control like wildfire. Douse it with a smile and a handshake and get on with your work. Criticizing will only jeopardize the situation further.

We all make mistakes. We all get upset and angry. We all have shortcomings. So, we have no right to be critical of others. Before pointing our finger at someone, we should first look within.

Criticism even when constructive still has a negative connotation. If it is necessary to offer constructive criticism, as during performance appraisal time, it should never be done publicly. In private, behind closed doors, is the best way.

By disrespecting others, you disrespect yourself. You attract negativity once you spew negativity about someone. Respect yourself by respecting others. In the workplace, if you criticize your co-workers, you will end up disrupting the atmosphere and spoiling everyone's mood. By not being critical and having solid bonding with everyone, you will sparkle like a solitary star.

Action Points

Assume positive intent:

1. Depersonalize other people's actions.
2. Train yourself to become realistic.
3. If you can't make a person's day, don't spoil it for them.

Offer constructive feedback, if necessary:

1. Focus on behaviour, not character.
2. Offer solutions to problems.
3. Choose the right time and place.

Focus on your own growth:

1. Understand what triggers you to criticize others.
2. Reflect on your own shortcomings.
3. Always express yourself assertively, not aggressively.

Remember,

Assess your own character before judging another's.

86

Be Joyful

When you are joyful, when you say yes to life and have fun and project
positivity all around you, you become a sun in the center of every
constellation, and people want to be near you.

—Shannon L. Alder

If you are joyful, you can infuse enthusiasm into even the most sombre environment. Atul Shah possessed this unique gift. During my tenure as a branch manager in a private bank in Mumbai, Shah excelled as a relationship manager. I never witnessed a moment of dejection or sadness in him. His boundless energy was contagious and uplifted everyone around him.

One incident stands out vividly. We were racing against a tight deadline, and the pressure was immense. The office was a tense hive of activity, filled with the rhythmic tapping of keyboards and punctuated by frustrated sighs.

Then Shah arrived. His infectious optimism, coupled with a radiant smile and encouraging words, transformed the atmosphere. He distributed candy, shared lighthearted jokes and offered assistance with a cheerful demeanor. His impromptu performance of a song further elevated everyone's spirits.

With renewed energy and a positive outlook, the team pressed on with their work.

About Being Joyful:

If you are happy, you are engaged. Your productivity is higher. When you are joyful, you are stress-free. Imagine the difference between working under stress and working stress-free. Those working under stress are bound to commit errors, miss deadlines and feel disengaged but those who are free of stress will do quality work, meet deadlines and face all challenges with energy and enthusiasm.

When you work joyfully, you create a positive atmosphere. In a positive atmosphere, working becomes a treat. Everyone wants to give off their best because it is fun to work. It's unlike in a negative atmosphere, when it is a burden to work. Joy is contagious. Just like someone's negativity gets rubbed off on you, the same happens with being happy also. So your joyfulness will affect others in a huge positive way. A positive work culture is cultivated by individuals who bring joy to their roles. Their enthusiasm is a magnet for productivity and job satisfaction. In contrast, negativity can create a toxic environment that hinders progress.

If you are unable to find joy in your work, either quit or make your work joyful. Once you make your work joyful, you will work joyfully. You will be able to connect well with your colleagues and they will reciprocate in the same way.

While challenges, deadlines and fatigue are inevitable in any job, a positive outlook can transform how we handle them. A joyful approach empowers us to navigate stress effectively.

How do you make your work joyful? Identify at least one activity which brings you joy. Back when I was a part of the corporate workplace, it was always my effort that whoever dropped by to see me in my office, whether my team members, my boss, peers, other colleagues, clients, etc., I would want them to leave with smiles on their faces, no matter which mood they came in with.

What's that one thing at work which brings you joy? Find it.

Action Points

Focus on the positive:

1. Find meaning in your work.
2. Celebrate your daily accomplishments.
3. Appreciate the positive aspects of your work environment.

Build genuine connections:

1. Bond well with your teammates.
2. Be generous with your compliments.
3. Get to know your colleagues on a personal level.

Personalize your space:

1. Create a workspace that inspires you and makes you happy.
2. Incorporate nature, like plants or natural light.
3. Maintain a neat and tidy workstation.

Remember,

Happiness is a choice. Choose to be joyful.

87

Don't Forget Your Manners

It is a wise thing to be polite; consequently,
it is a stupid thing to be rude.

—Arthur Schopenhauer

A loud, aggressive voice shattered the calm. I came out of my office to see what the matter was. Topiwala, a new client whom we had on-boarded recently, was clearly unhappy with something, and he was yelling at the young clerk, Nisha.

Visibly shaken, Nisha was doing her best to apologize and rectify the situation, but Topiwala was in no mood to listen. He continued his tirade, his words laced with sarcasm and condescension.

I felt a surge of anger bubbling within me. 'How dare he talk to my team member like this?' I told myself. I wanted to step in and defend Nisha and put the customer in his place. And I was almost ready to do this because Topiwala's behaviour was getting even more atrocious with every passing moment and Nisha, unable to bear it, had started crying.

But I held myself. My mother's words came rushing into my mind. 'Manners are a mirror reflecting your own character, not theirs.' Taking a deep breath, I walked towards the counter.

'Excuse me, sir,' I said politely. 'I couldn't help but overhear. Perhaps we can find a solution that works for everyone.'

This approach surprised Topiwala. His voice lowered automatically. I escorted him to my office, offered him water and tea, listened to him and then proposed actions which he accepted. He left my office much calmer.

Nisha came to thank me for rescuing her. She said, 'How could you keep your cool, sir?'

I said, 'Sometimes, the best response to bad manners is to remind others how good manners work. It may not change them, but it defines who you are.'

About Not Forgetting Your Manners

Good manners speak volumes about the kind of person you are. In office, you will have people of varied dispositions and backgrounds. There might be misunderstandings, disagreements and conflicts, leading to the flaring of tempers, and yelling, screaming and the use of cuss words. Let whoever wants to behave in this fashion do so, but you shouldn't. Just because someone forgets his or her manners, it doesn't mean you should forget yours too.

Remember the words of former American president Theodore Roosevelt, 'Politeness is a sign of dignity, not subservience.' Ignore perceptions of fear or submission. Maintain your composure and good manners.

Good manners at the workplace are the foundation of strong and positive relations with your co-workers. Also, pay heed to the code of conduct in place in the office. Compromising on any of these can hinder your progress and give you a bad reputation. Getting rid of a bad reputation is almost impossible because a perception gets built about you and once you are perceived as a toxic person, no one will want to deal with you.

Be very careful while dealing with your co-workers. Make use of the five magical words that we all learnt in kindergarten. *Please. Thank-you. Sorry. Excuse me. You're welcome.* They are as evergreen today as they were then. They have the power to create pathways when the going gets tough. They can ease difficulties at work. They can help you to overcome obstacles.

With good manners, you will appear to be in greater command. And they cost you nothing. Those who display rudeness have lost control over themselves as well as the situation. It's not only a professional mistake to be rude, it's like committing professional suicide.

Establish your credentials at the workplace, by displaying immaculate manners.

Action Points

Be mindful and considerate:

1. Pause and think before you speak.
2. Be aware of your body language.
3. Smile. It costs nothing, but creates a powerful impact.

Practise basic courtesies:

1. Be punctual always.
2. Use polite language.
3. Acknowledge others.

Adapt your manners to the situation:

1. Respect cultural differences.
2. In formal settings, be formal.
3. Become a role model for others to emulate.

Remember,

Your manners are a mirror reflecting your character.

88

Be Tactful

*Tact is the ability to step on a man's toes
without messing up the shine on his shoes.*

—Harry Truman

The new project manager, Ajay Kumar, felt the weight of
responsibility settle upon his shoulders. Assigned to collaborate
with a team known for their strong personalities and differing
work styles, he knew smooth sailing wasn't guaranteed.

He went to seek advice from his mentor, who simply told
him, 'Ajay, be tactful.'

Kumar's first meeting with the team was chaotic. The
room buzzed with passionate arguments, each member fiercely
defending their vision for the project. The atmosphere grew
tense, threatening to derail progress before it had even begun.

Kumar recalled his mentor's words, *be tactful*. So, instead of
silencing anyone or imposing his own viewpoint, he employed
a subtle approach.

'Thank you all for sharing your valuable perspectives,' he
started, acknowledging everyone's contribution and creating a
sense of inclusivity. 'It's clear we all have a vested interest in this

project's success. Perhaps, before diving into specifics, we can discuss our common goals and identify where our visions overlap.'

By tactfully shifting the focus to shared objectives instead of individual differences, Kumar fostered a sense of unity. The team, encouraged by this approach, began identifying common ground and building upon it. They were able to weave their diverse ideas into a cohesive plan, all because Kumar was tactful.

About Being Tactful:

Tactfulness is a must-have skill in the workplace. You should train yourself to say the right thing in the right situation. You should also avoid saying something incorrect, when you are tempted to do so. You must handle the situation in such a way that you are able to express your point without upsetting or annoying anyone.

If you aren't tactful, you will have trouble maintaining relationships and your ability to learn will also get hampered. Samuel Butler said, 'Silence is not always tact and it is tact that is golden, not silence.' Imagine how powerful a tool is tact. Familiarity does not equate to informality. Even long-standing relationships require tact and consideration.

With practice and good judgement, you can become tactful. You should have skills like emotional intelligence, empathy, politeness and good listening. Many confuse tact with lying. It is not the case. Lying is bad. Tact is good. Tact is the ability to be assertive without upsetting the other person.

A win-win outcome is always the best solution. Both the parties involved are happy that they got what they wanted the most by letting go of what wasn't that important. Tactfulness is a great asset to have when you are negotiating or you have to deliver some bad news or critical feedback.

In the workplace, cultivating relationships is important; tactfulness helps in preserving existing relationships and building new ones. Let me give an example. If you must tell a team member that he is not doing enough during the day, you don't go and say, 'You are slow.' This approach can damage the relationship because the team member might get offended and withdraw into a shell. Instead, you can say, 'Let me show you ways to improve efficiency.'

As you grow in your professional career, tact and diplomacy will become more important. Without these qualities, you cannot have credibility. Be open-minded, tolerant and patient and you will have no trouble in mastering tact.

Action Points

Think twice before speaking:

1. Take a moment to consider the situation.
2. Choose your words carefully.
3. Focus on the issue, not the person.

Be empathetic and respectful:

1. Agree to disagree.
2. Make use of the pause button when emotions get heated.
3. Listen more, talk less.

Find common ground:

1. Look for areas of agreement.
2. Offer ways and ideas to move forward.
3. Be open to compromise.

Remember,

Tact is the hallmark of character, maturity and professionalism, distinguishing you from the crowd.

89

Choose Your Battles Wisely

Choose your battles wisely. After all, life isn't measured by how many times you stood up to fight. It's not winning battles that makes you happy, but it's how many times you turned away and chose to look into a better direction. Life is too short to spend it on warring. Fight only the most, most, most important ones, let the rest go.

—C. JoyBell C.

The air crackled with the intensity of a heated debate. Maurice Tate, known for his outspoken nature, found himself in a disagreement with his colleague, Bashir Gaya, about the marketing strategy for their upcoming product launch. Their viewpoints were poles apart, and tension was building up.

Fuelled by passion for his vision, Tate felt compelled to defend his ideas aggressively. He was ready to fight the battle, come what may. But as he began formulating his counterarguments, he paused, remembering his ex-boss's words: 'Silence speaks volumes, and choosing your battles wisely can win you the war.'

So, Tate opted for a different approach. Instead of escalating the argument, he acknowledged Gaya's perspective. 'I fully understand your concerns, Bashir,' he said calmly. 'Perhaps we can combine the strengths of our ideas to create a more comprehensive strategy.'

This shift in approach defused the tension. Gaya, surprised by Tate's acknowledgement, responded positively. Together, they brainstormed, and devised a strategy that incorporated the best aspects of both approaches, creating a solution stronger than either of their individual ideas.

By choosing his battles wisely, Tate realized how he had successfully navigated a tense situation that could have spiralled into chaos. Also, it yielded a better outcome and strengthened his professional relationship with Gaya.

Winning the war isn't about dominating every battle.

About Choosing Your Battles Wisely:

Choosing your battles wisely is an art. There will be many instances in life and in the workplace when you will be tempted to speak your mind at the cost of your own reputation. But knowing when to speak your mind makes you a professional and is the way to success, both in your personal and professional life.

Dealing with people can be challenging, frustrating, irritating and stressful, but you can't escape them. At work or outside it, you will keep encountering them, unless you choose to withdraw from the world and become a hermit. So, how we handle people and situations defines our personality.

You will face all sorts of scenarios. A peer may behave with you as if he or she is your boss, your boss may give you a difficult time, your junior may defy you or a co-worker may misbehave with you. Now, if you were to get into a fight with all of them, then you would be a wreck.

Discernment is the key. Should you get involved or give the situation a miss? Is it worth your time and energy to fight such issues or is there a better, more professional way to tackle such matters? There is definitely a better, more professional way to handle all the four scenarios I have mentioned, rather than getting into a fight.

But should you always be silent and refrain from taking action? That's not the right tactic either. When it comes to your principles, values and ethics, you should not back down or keep quiet. On such occasions, you should raise your voice. Make your point. Spell out what you mean. Elaborate, clarify, explain. But do it, without getting into an argumentative tone. Or fighting.

So, do not fuss over small stuff, silly things and ordinary issues, because when the time comes, when you must get an urgent thing done or get your way when something is important, then you will face roadblocks. Your reputation will precede you.

Therefore, choosing your battles wisely is the cleverest thing you can do in the workplace.

Action Points

Identify what matters most:

1. Reflect on what truly matters to you in life and at work.
2. Seek alternative conflict resolution strategies instead of escalating disagreements into arguments.
3. Consider the long-term impact.

Be considerate:

1. Consider that (in case of an argument/disagreement), both parties could be right.
2. Mind your own business all the time.
3. Don't try to address sensitive issues in the heat of the moment or in a public setting.

Know when to walk away or compromise:

1. If a situation doesn't directly violate your core values, let it go.

2. If there's no chance of a positive conversation, let it go.
3. Disengage from unproductive arguments.

Remember,

The outcome of a battle rarely defines one's peace of mind.

90

Never Give Excuses

*He that is good for making excuses is seldom good
for anything else.*
—Benjamin Franklin

Purohit Raj was assigned a project by his manager. He worked hard on it but multiple stakeholders were involved and certain deliverables could not be submitted on time. As a result, an important milestone was not achieved.

Purohit's manager, infuriated and perturbed, called for him. As the manager began venting out his frustration, Purohit went on the defensive and immediately started giving excuses. 'It isn't my fault,' he said. 'IT and Marketing did not deliver the requirements on time. What could I do?' This stance of his further upset the manager and he berated him.

Purohit came out of the manager's office, feeling upset. He was wondering what wrong he had done. He had worked hard, and the milestone was missed not because of his doing but because of dependency on other stakeholders. He sat at his desk, an emotional wreck, his face red with embarrassment.

A senior colleague, Narayanan, asked 'Purohit, tell me what happened in the manager's cabin.' Purohit narrated the entire incident. Narayanan chuckled. 'Never give excuses.'

'But I didn't, sir. I simply told him that missing the deadline was not my fault.'

'That's the excuse,' said the senior colleague.

'But how? Am I to be blamed in any way?'

'You are not to be blamed. But you are responsible. The project was assigned to you. So you were the owner.'

'I don't get you. If I am not to be blamed, how am I responsible?' Purohit asked.

'You are not to be blamed because the dependency was on other stakeholders, but you are responsible because you were the owner of the project. So, if the milestone was missed, the onus falls on you. You should not have given any excuse to the manager but instead, you should have accepted the responsibility for the delay, and explained the reasons for it.'

Purohit understood the significance of what Narayanan was saying and decided not to commit the mistake of giving excuses ever again.

About Never Giving Excuses:

Don't minimize your potential by giving excuses. The more excuses you make, the further you move away from your purpose.

Why do we make excuses? We do it to free ourselves from accountability. We don't want to take any blame or face the heat. We want to avoid uncomfortable situations. We need protection, to save face. We don't want anyone to point fingers at us.

We do not realize that our thought process is wrong. This flawed thinking is not going to benefit us in any way. We have become so used to making excuses, that we don't have to make much of an effort to come up with them. We will blame someone else, our team, the boss, the system, policies, the management. Or we will say, 'We don't have time.' Or, 'Why me?' Or, 'I don't have any resources.' Or 'I don't know' and many such lame reasons that make no sense.

Yes, there may be genuine reasons, at times, but that shouldn't be confused with excuses.

One example to highlight this:

Reason: I couldn't complete my target because the product was out of stock. I had buyers lined up though.

Excuse: No one picked up my calls.

By making excuses you are:

- limiting yourself
- playing it safe
- eroding your confidence
- inculcating a victim mentality
- creating a pattern of avoidance
- running away from challenges
- missing opportunities

By not making excuses, you will develop a winner's mindset which will turn you into a fine professional.

Action Points

Pre-empt excuses with proactive planning:

1. Anticipate potential roadblocks.
2. Develop contingency plans to address them.
3. Understand the difference between explanation and excuse, explain the situation and propose solutions.

Take a different view:

1. Never play the 'victim' card.
2. Focus not on mistakes, but on the learning gained from them.
3. Analyse and act.

Focus on deliverables:

1. Prioritize the delivery of results.
2. Acknowledge the problem and concentrate on rectification.
3. Ensure that correction/rectification is done on time.

Remember,

Explanations are acceptable, excuses are not.

91

Develop Influence

The greatest ability in business is to get along with others and to influence their actions.

—John Hancock

Jessica's story is a testament to the fact that influence doesn't require a title or a forceful personality.

A junior accountant at a prestigious financial firm, she felt that she was drowning in a sea of paperwork and uninspiring colleagues. The office buzzed with negativity. But she believed in the company's mission and knew the team was capable of more. So she decided not to succumb to cynicism.

She not only followed orders but went around asking questions, not hesitating even one bit. She delved deeper into the company's financial data, uncovering hidden inefficiencies and outdated processes. She identified problems and at the same time proposed solutions. Though no one paid much attention to her solutions, she persisted.

She built relationships with her co-workers by being an active listener. She listened to their frustrations, shared her research and insights, and encouraged collaboration. Slowly, but steadily, her quiet influence began to take root.

Word about her spread. People started approaching her for her views. She gave her suggestions. She outlined her ideas in meetings and discussions. She became a bridge between departments, fostering a culture of open communication and shared ownership.

Jessica's influence stemmed from her genuine interest in the work, her respect for her colleagues and her unwavering belief in the team's potential. She neither had any authority nor was she manipulative. By demonstrating the power of quiet competence and a genuine desire to see everyone succeed, she was able to develop influence.

About Developing Influence:

Influence is the art of inspiring action. It's about connecting with others on a deeper level, understanding their motivations and guiding them towards a shared goal. True leaders are skilled influencers who build trust, foster collaboration and create a positive impact.

To influence effectively, one must prioritize empathy, transparency and authenticity. By showcasing vulnerability and leading by example, you inspire loyalty and dedication from your team. Remember, influence is not about control but about empowerment. It's about creating an environment where people feel valued, heard and motivated to contribute their best.

Master this skill and unlock a world of opportunities. It can propel your career to new heights.

Action Points

Become a communication master:

1. Hone both your verbal and non-verbal communication skills.
2. Use persuasive language that resonates with confidence.
3. Project an overall positive and approachable demeanour.

Build relationships and credibility:

1. Get to know your co-workers.
2. Prioritize team building.
3. Be reliable; follow through on commitments.

Become a champion for others:

1. People are naturally drawn to those who champion their causes and advocate their success.
2. Identify opportunities to support your colleagues and peers.
3. Celebrate their achievements and offer help when needed.

Remember,

Influence isn't about power; it's about connection. Genuine interest in your team and a shared sense of purpose are the true foundations of leadership.

92

Inspire Development

Before you are a leader, success is all about growing
yourself. When you become a leader, success is
all about growing others.

—Jack Welch

I had a team leader, Aarez Khan, who saw the potential in everyone and not just their technical expertise. He was every inch a true leader. He would often engage his team in casual conversations, asking them about their childhood dreams and passions.

One day, during a particularly mundane project review meeting, he saw Vani, a new recruit, doodling intricate sketches on her notepad. After the meeting, he approached her. 'Those are amazing drawings,' he said. Vani blushed, surprised that her Team Leader had noticed and genuinely complimented her.

Over the next few weeks, Khan continued to engage Vani, not just about the project development but also about her artistic aspirations. He encouraged her to participate in a bank-wide talent show, a suggestion she initially dismissed because of self-doubt. But Khan's persistent encouragement made her overcome her fear and she showcased her artwork alongside colleagues who sang, danced and performed various other activities.

Vani's participation, inspired by Khan's belief in her, ignited a dormant spark within the company's culture. Hidden talents suddenly came to the fore and soon the office walls were adorned with paintings by different employees. Creative energy ran through the entire organization and the workplace became more vibrant and innovative.

Inspiring development doesn't require a flamboyant personality or a special title. Like Khan, all that it requires is genuine care, encouragement and a firm belief in the potential that lies within everyone.

About Inspiring Development:

Developing others is one of the highest acts one can do. It is a selfless task. The benefits of helping and developing others are huge. Adaptability is one skill your team will instantly acquire. So, under pressure, they won't crack. They will improvise.

Let the organization take its own steps to develop employees. But you must take it upon yourself to develop them. Be proactive and work on your team members. Know what their strengths and weaknesses are. And then chalk out an action plan to work on their weaknesses, but spend more time on strengthening their strengths and utilizing their strengths in different situations.

Create mock scenarios, give them role playing activities, read inspirational passages to them daily. This could encourage them to read. Additionally, debate with them on different topics, guide them to find solutions to problems, make them think creatively and critically, provide qualitative feedback, coach and mentor them.

You do a great thing when you inspire others to do great things. You develop when you start developing others. Performance gets impacted positively and in today's world, the organization must keep outperforming its own performance. In the workplace, you should expect the unexpected. If you develop others, they will be able to manage the unexpected. Otherwise, things will turn from bad to worse.

Anyone who can bring out an individual's potential is a leader. Focus on doing that with your team members. Excuses like *I am not here to develop others* or *They should develop themselves on their own* or *It is HR's job to develop employees* should be discarded from your mind. Excuses are the hallmark of a defeatist attitude.

A winner's mindset is different. Believing in yourself is the most important requirement. And believing in yourself will make you turn your attention to helping and supporting and developing others because, by doing that, you sharpen your winner's abilities more. Multiply the talents and skills of your team members and co-workers and see how it translates into your growth and that of the company.

Action Points

Spark curiosity:

1. Foster open-mindedness to enhance learning and knowledge acquisition.
2. Introduce challenges that stretch abilities.
3. Share inspiring stories of development and overcoming obstacles.

Make the work environment supportive:

1. Support risk-taking and view mistakes as learning opportunities.

2. Remove barriers.
3. Encourage a growth-oriented approach.

Personalize the development journey:

1. Align development initiatives with individual goals and aspirations, to maximize engagement and impact.
2. Help people identify their strengths and areas for growth.
3. Create individualized learning plans.

Remember,

Shift your focus from limitations to limitless possibilities.

This is the catalyst for extraordinary growth.

93

Pay Attention to Detail

The simple act of paying attention can take you a long way.
— Keanu Reeves

Farida was a whiz at churning out code. She wrote scripts faster than anyone. But her presentations, though visually stunning, contained incorrect numbers here and there, and her emails, while technically sound, lacked context.

If any colleague of hers were to point out any flaws to her, she would attribute it to nitpicking. She thought that they were envious of her. It wasn't until a major campaign launch that she realized the true importance of paying attention to detail. Her expertly coded email automation went live, bombarding customers with a flurry of messages—many even congratulating them on non-existent purchases. Chaos reigned supreme, and the PR department had a tough time settling complaints.

Demoralized with the incident, she rushed to a colleague, the ever reliable, ever helpful Vishnu Prasad. He was a master in his work, who never neglected a detail. It was said that if Prasad had worked on a document or a presentation then there was no need to double-check it. So careful and meticulous was he with details.

When Farida narrated her story, Prasad did not chastise her for her speed. He said how fast or slow you work is up to you, but attention to detail is important. If a surgeon or a pilot were to neglect details, it could lead to disaster. In your case, a misplaced comma could mislead readers, a forgotten detail in a presentation could raise doubts, and an unchecked fact could lead to catastrophic outcomes.

'Details tell the true story,' he added. 'A single flaw can distract from the whole. Every piece matters.'

Farida learnt an important lesson that day. She took Prasad's words to heart. She reduced her speed, began double-checking her work, sought feedback, added context to her code, scrutinized every detail and, whenever possible, requested Prasad to review the text before hitting 'Send'.

Detail-oriented focus is essential for achieving exceptional results.

About Paying Attention to Detail:

You cannot have a strong work ethic if you do not pay attention to detail. Excellence doesn't come by accident. Do not confuse excellence with perfection. To me, perfection is unattainable. Being the best version of yourself always, that should be your goal. So, every day, keep working on the masterpiece that you are, and therefore the work that you create should also not be less than a masterpiece.

Paying attention to detail is the single most essential requirement for excelling. When you neglect to pay attention, you tend to get careless, and carelessness indicates lack of interest, integrity and involvement. The result will lack quality as there will be no accuracy or precision.

In many jobs, one error can prove costly. Unless contracts, policies and procedures benefit from attention to detail, the organization will be vulnerable to legal claims and challenges. Ben Hopgood, a content marketing manager with Test Partnership, refers to attention to detail as 'A person's behavioural propensity towards thoroughness, accuracy, and consistency when accomplishing tasks.'

You will be able to manage your work more efficiently because you will be able to spot errors early on if you are methodical. This approach will reduce rework which is a major problem area in many organizations. Your style will also rub off on your co-workers and they will also start paying attention to detail which can improve the output of your department.

You can develop this skill by being more organized and observant, managing time effectively, prioritizing, analysing and single tasking. Paying attention to details shows that you take pride in what you do and are committed to quality and will not settle for anything less. That's the hallmark of a true professional.

Action Points

Slow down and be present:

1. Don't rush through tasks.
2. Actively focus on what you are doing.
3. Get people to check, check and check again.

Develop active observation skills:

1. Create your own quality control procedures.
2. Train yourself to notice not only the big picture but also the finer points.
3. Be mindful of potential inconsistencies or errors.

Embrace checklists and systems:

1. Provide or insist on having the right tools.
2. Create checklists for tasks that require precision.
3. Utilize technology like reminders and note-taking apps, to stay organized and on track.

Remember,

Small oversights can have catastrophic consequences.

94

Communicate Well

Communicate in a respectful manner—don't just tell your team members what you want, but explain to them why.

—Jeffrey Morales

In my early days as a banker, when I was managing a branch in a private bank in Mumbai, an incident occurred that highlights how essential it is to communicate well.

The head teller at the branch was Farokh Irani. One of his assistants was Nazleen, a fresh graduate. Though new, she was as efficient as a Swiss watch. Transactions zipped through her fingers, numbers danced on the screen and receipts materialized in a blur.

Yet, customer satisfaction scores for her lane remained stubbornly low. She was puzzled as to why. She began observing Irani. He wasn't faster than her, but his interactions with customers crackled with warmth. He listened patiently to a retiree's concerns about online banking, calmly explaining each step. He would pacify flustered customers by asking clarifying questions and offering solutions.

One day, a frantic client rushed into Nazleen's lane, clutching a crumpled withdrawal slip. Nazleen, whose primary focus was speed, rattled off the standard verification questions. The client, on the verge of tears, stammered and fumbled. Nazleen got frustrated and looked around, trying to understand what she should do next.

Irani had seen Nazleen struggling. He stepped in at the right moment. In a calm and reassuring tone, he asked the client to repeat her request. She explained that she needed money urgently to buy medicines for her sick child and that she had forgotten her cheque book and wanted to make a withdrawal, using the withdrawal slip. After listening intently, he helped her navigate the system, while ensuring accuracy.

Nazleen thanked him for the support. Irani told her, 'Nazleen, it's not just about the transaction and the speed with which you execute it. It's more about understanding the client's needs and reassuring them.'

In the world of finance or anywhere, communicating well is the most important aspect. It helps to build trust.

About Communicating Well:

Clear and effective communication can pave the way for a productivity boost. Your personal and professional success depends largely upon how well you can communicate. Projects fail, deadlines get missed and conflicts happen because of poor communication skills.

Collaboration is the heartbeat of all organizations because it gives a sense of purpose to the employees as it creates a more cohesive and open workplace. But to collaborate in a powerful and impactful manner, communication is necessary. Any misunderstanding can lead to disastrous consequences.

There is a huge difference between communicating and communicating well. If you can communicate, you can get the work done, but if you are able to communicate well, you can work wonders. To communicate well, you need to connect well first. Bonding matters.

Effective communication hinges on understanding rather than eloquence. While strong speaking skills can influence, it's the ability to listen and comprehend that truly connects with an audience or team. Great communication is a combination of a message well spoken, well listened and well understood.

So, decide what and how you are going to speak and after you have finished, make sure that your message has been understood by recapping all that you have said and cross-checking with the team. And when you are the recipient, listen actively by paying full attention without interruption and disturbance and after the speaker has finished, clear your doubts, if any, immediately. How your body responds while communicating is equally important. Positive body language plays a critical role.

Action Points

Be clear and concise:

1. Avoid jargon and technical terms that might confuse your audience.
2. Get your message across in a way that is easy to understand.
3. Organize your thoughts logically.

Communication is a two-way street:

1. Pay close attention to what the other person is saying.
2. Ask clarifying questions to ensure understanding.
3. Avoid interrupting.

Choose the right communication channel:

1. Hold face to face meetings.
2. Anticipate potential conflicts and handle them tactfully.
3. Use silence as a conversation tool.

Remember,

> The measure of successful communication lies
> in the depth of understanding achieved.

95

Enhance Your Personal Brand

Brand yourself for the career you want,
not the job you have.

—Dan Schawbel

Hidden away in her tiny studio, Yesha, a talented young fashion designer, meticulously crafted stunning garments. But despite her pouring her heart and soul into each piece, her designs remained unknown. Local boutiques wouldn't give her a chance because they catered only to established names. She felt discouraged, her talent trapped in obscurity.

Over a cup of coffee, when Yesha confided to her closest friend, Insia, the latter suggested personal branding. At first, Yesha hesitated, seeing it as self-promotion rather than artistry. But Insia convinced her that personal branding was the need of the hour and if she didn't do it, she would remain obscure.

Yesha embraced the idea and, with Insia's help, created a website showcasing her work, its influences and her design philosophy. She built a social media presence, sharing her latest sketches, behind-the-scenes glimpses and engaging with potential clients. Within a few months, her situation changed.

People began responding to her authenticity and passion. Bloggers featured her work and she got interviewed on several platforms. Impressed by her online presence, boutiques contacted her. Yesha's personal brand, built on her design philosophy and artistic vision, became the connection between her enormous talent and the world.

She finally got the recognition that she deserved. This proves that a powerful personal brand can uncover hidden talents and propel individuals to extraordinary heights.

About Enhancing Your Personal Brand:

Your reputation and your personal brand are two distinctive things. How others see you is your reputation. How you want others to see you is your personal brand. Personal branding is vital for progress and growth. It shows what value adds you bring to the organization and what your USP is.

Only when you are different, will you make a difference. Personal branding is all about making a difference.

Catherine Kaputa, in her book, *The New Brand You* says, 'Being better is often not enough. You need a different better. Your positioning is your differentiator.' So, how you position, project and present yourself, can make a huge difference to your personal brand. What is that one skill, quality or trait that is unique to you? Magnify it.

Branding needs visibility. First make yourself visible. Create a space, carve a niche and be known, and then align your values with what your organization stands for. Establish who you are and what your uniqueness is in the minds of others. Once you have done this, do not send out confusing signals by acting in a way that conflicts with your personal brand.

In the workplace and in life in general, it is perception that matters the most. More than reality. What people think of you carries more weight than what you do. So, creating a brand identity is an essential requirement if you are aspiring for higher levels in your company.

Visibility and credibility are the cornerstones of a powerful personal brand. They unlock countless opportunities and set you apart from the competition. By clearly defining your unique value proposition, you can captivate your audience and accelerate your success.

Create impact, impression and influence with your personal branding.

Action Points

Craft a compelling narrative:

1. Define and articulate your unique value proposition by identifying your core strengths, values and contributions.
2. Reflect on your skills, experiences and passions.
3. Craft a message that your target audience understands.

Engage and network strategically:

1. Actively participate in online communities and industry events.
2. Connect with people who share your interests and goals.
3. Be open to collaborating with others.

Build a robust online presence:

1. Audit and curate your online presence to align with your personal brand.
2. Showcase your achievements, skills and experience through impactful visuals and content.

3. Develop and maintain a consistent output of high-quality content to establish thought leadership in your field.

Remember,

Talent without visibility is potential unrealized.

96

Have a Work–Life Balance

You can't do a good job if your job is all you do.
—Katie Thurmes

Roohi, a rising star in the marketing department, thrived on the adrenaline of deadlines and the satisfaction of a flawless campaign launch. But for her relentless pursuit of success, she had to pay a heavy price. Her personal life was zero. Her apartment became an extension of the office, devoid of love, life and laughter.

Soon, her crazy working style led to her getting burnt out. She began losing her grip on her work, and whatever proposals she submitted were overlooked for those submitted by her peers. Her confidence began dwindling. Her colleague from another department ran into her one day in the lift. On hearing her out, he advised, work–life balance. 'If you don't set boundaries, you are going nowhere, Roohi.'

She decided to follow the advice. First, she started leaving work on time. Then, she rediscovered her passion for writing. Weekends were dedicated to creative writing classes. She began catching up with friends. Gradually, a sense of balance emerged.

Her creativity flourished, fuelled by new experiences and a relaxed mind.

Back at work, her renewed energy translated into exceptional ideas. She was back with a bang. She collaborated more effectively, her presentations brimmed with new-found enthusiasm. She called up her colleague to thank him for guiding her about the importance of work–life balance.

He said, 'Success isn't about a constant hustle. It is about creating a synergy between work and life.'

Prioritize your well-being so that you can give your work priority.

About Having a Work–Life Balance:

Mental and physical well-being is of utmost importance if you want to shine in the workplace. Without good health, your focus, concentration and willingness would not be of the required level and thus the quality of work will be affected.

A proper work–life balance gives you that edge. You are focused, energetic and raring to go. This enables you to give proper attention to work, thus boosting efficiency. When you work attentively, the chances of errors get minimized to almost negligible levels.

A study by Aviva says that employees are more attracted to work–life balance than to salary. Merely grinding away at your desk is not the way professionals work. Don't be bored and boring. When work becomes a mundane task, disengagement follows, often resulting in subpar performance. Work should be done with passion and fun and involvement.

If we balance work and life, there will be fewer health problems, which means fewer employees taking sick leave.

Employees will be more engaged. More mindfulness and fewer burnouts are the other two benefits.

So, if you are able to have a good work–life balance, you will be in robust health. Switch on–switch off mode is one way to balance work and other pursuits. Once your work hours are over, you should switch off and make time for your family and what you enjoy doing. Never carry office issues home and never bring domestic affairs to office. Learn to draw a line between the two.

When you can balance work with your life, you can motivate your team to do the same. But as Sadhguru says, 'There is no such thing as work and life, it is life and life. If your work is not life, I do not see why you should do it.'

Passion for one's work can often eliminate the need for strict work–life boundaries. However, when job satisfaction is lacking, maintaining a healthy equilibrium between professional and personal life becomes crucial.

Action Points

Set boundaries:

1. Carve out clear boundaries between your work and personal life.
2. Prioritize ruthlessly.
3. Learn to say no to extra tasks when your plate is full.

Practise time management:

1. Set specific work hours; avoid checking emails outside those hours.
2. Schedule time for what matters.
3. Don't leave your personal life to chance.

Know when to disconnect and recharge:

1. To prevent burnout, disconnect from work.
2. Take regular breaks.
3. Silence work notifications outside work hours.

Remember,

> Viewing work as a burden perpetuates a
> never-ending cycle of toil.

97

Volunteer

Volunteers do not necessarily have the time;
they just have the heart.
—Elizabeth Andrew

Natasha was the first in the marketing department to enlist her name for the company's new initiative, a monthly volunteer day.

She arrived early for the beach clean-up drive. Seeing the polluted shore, the impact of consumerism on the environment hit her hard. That day while filling bags with plastic waste, she resolved to participate in as many volunteer activities as she could.

Over the next few months, she made herself available for all the events that the company had organized: from planting trees at a local park to teaching art to children at the orphanage to sharing her ideas about the future with high school students.

What started as a duty became a passion.

She became an advocate for sustainable marketing practices, proposing campaigns that promoted eco-friendly products and educated consumers. Her colleagues, inspired by her volunteering spirit, started supporting her.

The company, once focused solely on profit, embraced environmental wellness. Natasha's volunteering drive fostered a sense of purpose and a renewed focus on corporate social responsibility.

About Volunteering:

These days most companies promote volunteerism. You should participate wholeheartedly in such initiatives. Volunteering programmes are linked with corporate social responsibility and reflect a business's accountability and commitment towards the wellness of society by undertaking various environmental and social measures.

By volunteering, you will be able to build a stronger sense of self, improve your well-being and get plenty of opportunities to learn and develop, deepen engagement and establish deep connections with co-workers and others in the community. Involve yourself in the volunteering programmes your company initiates. It will boost your morale and spirit and keep you purposeful. This will make you more engaged at work as you will love it more.

When you are volunteering, you get to practice valuable life skills without any pressure. These skills include interpersonal, communication, leadership, innovation, creativity, productivity, listening, adaptability, problem-solving, time management and many others. The experience you gain can translate well in the workplace. You bond well with your co-workers, your productivity goes up; volunteering can also help you advance your career.

For volunteering, you need only passion and positivity. If you have these two, you do not require anything else. You get a sense of fulfilment because of the feeling that you are doing something that is benefiting others.

If your workplace is not into volunteering, that shouldn't deter you from being a volunteer. You can do it on your own. Identify the skills that you have and the sharing of which can help co-workers and benefit the organization. Then start coaching and sharing your knowledge. In this way, your learning will also continue. You can also volunteer to help struggling employees and others who have a deadline to meet and are behind. Do not expect anything in return, no recognition, no sharing of credit. If you are looking for recognition, do not volunteer.

If you volunteer to do something then it should be selfless, just for the sake of helping, that's all.

Action Points

Become a volunteer champion:

1. Assess your community's needs.
2. Sponsor a cause or an individual.
3. Support struggling ex-employees.

Promote skill-based volunteering:

1. Highlight the benefits of skill-based volunteering for both employees and the community.
2. Leverage employee expertise to address non-profit needs through skills-based volunteering or pro bono projects. Share success stories from colleagues who have volunteered.

Organize a team volunteering event:

1. Rally your colleagues to participate.
2. Take the initiative and suggest a cause.
3. Your enthusiasm and initiative can inspire others.

Remember,

Volunteering transforms the ordinary into extraordinary.

98

Always Be Relaxed

Sometimes the most productive thing you can do is relax.
—Mark Black

Wendy worked under constant pressure. Every task was carefully planned. She would sit late hours at home drafting the emails, chugging coffee by the gallon. She found herself working round the clock, unable to relax.

This was her style of working when Naina Naik joined her team. Unlike her, Naik worked with an air of calm. She was like a saint, unfazed by what was going on around her. She never seemed to be in a hurry, and even took time for leisurely lunches.

At first, Wendy thought that Naik was lazy and uninterested in her work. But Naik consistently met her deadlines and was very competent. Intrigued, Wendy began observing her working style closely.

She saw that Naik did some breathing exercises quite often during the day, stretched every thirty to forty minutes, and was always non-judgmental. She applied the same techniques and became more mindful of her surroundings. Within a week, her frantic energy was overcome by a sense of calm.

She became more in control of herself, started enjoying her lunch breaks, and was able to connect with colleagues on a personal level. She mastered the art of serenity and was able to produce exceptional work, without looking hurried and haggard.

A relaxed mind isn't a sign of weakness but a key to increasing your productivity without disrupting your inner calm.

About Always Being Relaxed:

Relaxation is a necessity, not a luxury. It is the key to success. If you cannot stay calm and composed during highly intense moments or tough situations, you will crack; once the cracks appear, you start disintegrating.

Calmness of mind is the prerequisite for progress.

Anticipate the worst-case scenario when you are caught in a challenging and testing situation. Once you know what that is, you can reassure yourself that the situation can't get worse than this, and your mind will be able to think of ways to tackle the obstacles. Knowing the worst-case scenario, you can tell your mind to relax. And your mind will get the message.

There are many strategies to help you relax. You can use some of them at the workplace. The best and easiest among them is controlled breathing. You can do it while sitting at your desk or workstation. Stretching is another way to relax. Just stand up and move your arms and legs and that's it. You can also try visualization. Imagine something nice and interesting, something that you love and enjoy, and you will feel good and relaxed.

In a workplace, it is easier to deal with people who are relaxed and in control of themselves and their emotions and the situation. No one likes to interact with a co-worker who gets cranky and angry because of work pressure, because they worsen the situation. A relaxed person can release the physical and mental tension accumulated in the body and can think more clearly and make better decisions. He or she will have a more positive outlook on life.

Being relaxed helps you to achieve a lot more. Solutions to problems will emerge, you will be able to focus better, you will feel revitalized and your relationship with co-workers will improve.

Action Points

Master your morning routine:

1. Start your day well; a good start sets the tone for the rest of the day.
2. Establish a morning routine that promotes calmness.
3. Take control of your morning so you feel centred.

Be mindful throughout the day:

1. Practise breathing exercises.
2. Take regular breaks.
3. Make use of mindfulness apps.

Remember that not everything is about you:

1. Understand perspectives.
2. Manage your expectations.
3. Don't be afraid to ask for help, if needed.

Remember,

Serenity is power. A calm mind can weather any storm.

99

Make the Right Connections

Know where you want to go and make sure the right people
know about it.

—Meredith Mahoney

Deep in the forest there lived a badger called Bob. He prided himself on his self-sufficiency. He built elaborate tunnels, stocked them with the finest berries and kept to himself. But as winter came, and the berry supply dwindled, Bob realized that survival wouldn't come from hoarding alone.

Bob spoke to Pipkin, the squirrel, who often used to pass by his burrow. She bartered information for favours. She knew who had the best acorn stashes and the warmest nesting spots. So, Bob struck a deal with her. Pipkin would share her network in exchange for Bob's winter stash.

Pipkin introduced Bob to Ollie, the wise old owl. Ollie taught Bob about the hidden honeycombs in the trees. She connected him with Belinda, the beaver, who offered access to an underwater haven rich with juicy fish. Bob, once a solitary badger, became part of a vibrant network.

The winter passed peacefully because Bob's burrow overflowed with food. He learnt that security and success don't come from isolation, but from cooperation and connection. By building relationships and making the right connections, Bob was able to thrive.

About Making the Right Connections:

Tim Sanders, a renowned author, speaker and former Yahoo! executive, famously stated, 'Your network is your net worth'. In today's interconnected world, who you know often determines your professional trajectory. While expertise is crucial, strategic connections can amplify your impact and open doors to unprecedented opportunities.

Your career advancement is largely in your own hands. While others can offer support, the onus is on you to identify key stakeholders within your organization. Building relationships with your manager, their superiors and the broader leadership team is crucial for career growth. Strategic networking can provide the momentum you need to soar.

Visibility is essential, but understanding your audience is paramount. Building strong relationships with key stakeholders is the cornerstone of career success. Cultivating these connections is a skill every professional must master.

Be outgoing. If you are an introvert, you will have to change because unless you reach out to people, you can't build connections within the organization. Look out for common interests. When I was working, I was able to bond with my bosses, because I identified a common thread between us. One boss loved books and I too am fond of books, so I could connect with him. One was a traveller and that was a shared interest between us. One was spiritual, and I too, am inclined towards spirituality: so we could relate with each other.

Your personal brand gets a boost, you attract plenty of opportunities, exchange of ideas and knowledge happens, you develop long-lasting relationships, you gain a different outlook towards work and life, these are some of the major benefits arising out of making the right connections.

Get ready to become more competitive and in demand by establishing connections with relevant people both inside and outside the organization.

Action Points

Cultivate genuine interest:

1. Prioritize active listening and empathetic communication. Be outgoing.
2. Focus on getting to know others.

Build relationships, not only networks:

1. Provide value.
2. Check-in with important contacts.
3. Look for ways to offer value.

Seek out quality interactions:

1. Don't just connect with people in your immediate circle.
2. Broaden your network.
3. Expose yourself to diverse perspectives and potential collaborators.

Remember,

Deepen connections beyond the surface.

100

Be a Comfort Zone for Others

Cure sometimes, treat often, comfort always.

—Hippocrates

Laila was like a ray of shine. The office dazzled because of her presence. Whenever she found colleagues upset, heartbroken, disappointed, depressed or frustrated, she would cheer them up.

Once when our coworker Disha's proposal was rejected by a big client, she was so dejected that we thought she would crumble, but Laila encouraged her in her usually fantastic way.

She brewed Disha a cup of her favourite lemon–mint tea. Then she pulled up a chair and sat next to Disha, not to dissect the proposal, but to listen. Disha poured out her frustration, the fear of letting down the team, the sting of rejection, the embarrassment. Laila, a skilled listener, didn't interrupt; she only nodded her head and occasionally said, 'I understand' or 'I get your point.'

When Disha finished talking, a change came over her face. Laila told her about her strengths, her insightful ideas and past accomplishments. Disha felt better. Laila suggested a brainstorming session on how the proposal could be improved.

Disha's despair dissipated. A spark of determination was lit within her. The next day, she presented a revised proposal, which wasn't just better, but addressed the client's concerns so well that they were delighted.

Disha, forever grateful, realized that Laila was a comfort zone, a safe place to go to in order to be heard.

Illuminate the darkest hours of others with your compassion.

About Being a Comfort Zone for Others:

Things can go wrong despite taking all precautions. But if and when they do, it is not the end of the world. People around you will make mistakes, take wrong decisions, fumble, fall and fail. When we goof up, we want someone to have our back. Someone who can give us the comfort of hope. Someone with whom we can talk freely about our issues, our insecurities and our lost confidence. And if we don't find someone with whom we can share our troubles, our anxiety can multiply.

Be that someone. Be a comfort zone for those who are struggling with their problems. You will be like an oasis for such people. By letting them come to you, in a free state of mind, unbothered about being judged or penalized, they will feel lighter and relaxed.

Hear them out, console them, motivate and encourage them, and drive them to move forward by telling them to forget the past, but learn from it. Your task is to provide comfort, not drive away their fears. As John Collins said, 'Don't try to make people's fear "go away" as that is not your job. Fear belongs to the person in whom it resides. It is not yours to fix.'

Don't solve their problems, guide them to do it themselves. Emphasize quality and focus, target the performance and not the performer. When you do this and do it consistently in the workplace, you not only create a positive image about yourself, but you also make the working environment better and the team more cohesive.

Action Points

Be warm and welcoming:

1. Use positive and inclusive language.
2. Be non-judgmental.
3. Listen, listen, listen.

Be understanding:

1. See things from others' viewpoints.
2. Be patient with their anxieties or vulnerabilities.
3. Validate their feelings without trying to fix their problems.

Offer encouragement:

1. Develop strategies to provide reassurance during difficult times.
2. Be a source of encouragement by believing in their capabilities.
3. Focus on their strengths and potential.

Remember,

> Be an island of refuge for those who have
> nowhere to go when disaster strikes them.

Acknowledgements

First and foremost, a big hug to Afsar, my brother, for being a rock of support, and thanks to his amazing team at Exceed, especially Tanvi, for their invaluable logistical assistance.

My parents have been my guiding stars, their blessings illuminating my path. My sisters, Yasmeen and Zarin, my sister-in-law, Sabrin, and all the children of my family—especially Saamish and Insia—have been my cheerleaders, constantly motivating me. I want to express my sincere gratitude to my wife, Farhat, for being the first reader of my manuscript. Her relentless support and insightful feedback were invaluable.

I am indebted to my senior colleague, Ashok, and friends Vijay, Dipan and Onkar, for their encouragement and constructive criticism. A special thanks to my nephew, Akif, for his fresh perspective. Deepak, a gifted writer himself, and Mudit, a true gem, deserve special recognition for gracing my book with their forewords. Their words of wisdom have elevated this work to new heights. I am eternally grateful to all the authors whose books have inspired and informed my writing. To my juniors, peers and bosses, especially Yasmine, Chetan, Mardood, Laxman, Nasser, Shafeqa and KK, thank you for being a constant source of learning and growth. I would also like to mention Farokh Mistry, an expert banker, a thorough gentleman and a guiding force for me.

Finally, a standing ovation to the editorial team at Penguin Random House India—Radhika, Cynthia and Aninda—for their expertise and dedication in shaping this book into its final form. Their contributions have been instrumental in enhancing its value.

To everyone who has touched my life and contributed to this book, thank you from the bottom of my heart.

Bibliography

Books

Garton, E., & Mankins, M., *Time, Talent, Energy: Overcome Organizational Drag and Unleash Your Team's Productive Power*, Harvard Business Review Press, Boston, 2017.

Kopmeyer, M.R., *Thoughts to Build On*, Success Unlimited, Chicago, 1970.

Moussavi, M., *The High Achiever's Guide*, Mango Publishing, Coral Gables, 2019.

Maxwell, J., *The 17 Indisputable Laws of Teamwork*, Thomas Nelson, Nashville, 2000.

Miller, J., *QBQ!*, G.P. Putnam's Sons, New York, 2004.

Csikszentmihalyi, M., *Flow*, Harper & Row, New York, 1990.

Covey, S., *The 7 Habits of Highly Effective People*, Free Press, New York, 1989.

Tracy, B., *Victory!*, Thomas Nelson, Nashville, 2010.

Dweck, C., *Mindset*, Ballantine Books, New York, 2006.

Inamori, K., *A Compass to Fulfillment*, McGraw-Hill, New York, 2009.

Kraft, H., *Deep Kindness*, TarcherPerigee, New York, 2020.

Hallowell, E., *Shine*, Harvard Business Press, Boston, 2011.

Schwartz, D., *The Magic of Thinking Big*, Prentice Hall, Englewood Cliffs, 1959.

Jones, P., *Exactly What to Say*, Page Two, Vancouver, 2017.

Huntsman, J., *Winners Never Cheat*, Wharton School Publishing, Philadelphia, 2005.

Chidiac, D., *Who Says You Can't? You Do*, Harmony Books, New York, 2018.

Eurich, T., *Insight*, Crown Business, New York, 2017.

Hardy, B., *Will Power Doesn't Work*, Hachette Books, New York, 2018.

Grazer, B., & Fishman, C., *A Curious Mind*, Simon & Schuster, New York, 2015.

McKeown, G., *Essentialism*, Crown Business, New York, 2014.

Templar, R., *The Rules of Work*, Pearson Education, Harlow, 2003.

Grant, A., *Think Again*, Viking, New York, 2021.

Kaputa, C., *The New Brand You*, Nicholas Brealey Publishing, London, 2022.

Articles & Research Papers

Kurland, Nancy B., and Lisa Hope Pelled. *Passing the Word: Towards a Model of Gossip and Power in the Workplace. Academy of Management Review*, April 2000.

HBR Surveys

Feser, Claudio. *When Execution Isn't Enough: Decoding Inspirational Leadership*. McKinsey & Co.

Work-Life Boundary. Aviva Study.

Learning Mindset Action Plan. Richardson Consulting Group.

Online References

'Becoming an Active Listener', *Wayne State University*, 13 May 2013, https://wayne.edu/learning-communities/pdf/becomingactive-listener-13.pdf

Agarwal, R., *Forbes, www.forbes.com*

'11 Helpful Strategies for Navigating Office Politics', *Forbes Human Resources Council*, 2 February 2021, https://www.forbes.com/councils/forbeshumanresourcescouncil/2021/02/02/11-helpful-strategies-for-navigating-office-politics/

'Managing Energy at Work', *Zapier*, *https://zapier.com/blog/managing-energy-at-work/*

Bickersteth, D., *LinkedIn*

Boitnott, K., *LinkedIn*

Yanus, M., *LinkedIn*

C, J., *LinkedIn*

Jayaram, M., *LinkedIn*

'Defying the Odds', *Ben Weinberg*, 6 May 2018, https://benjweinberg.com/2018/05/06/defyingthe-odds/

'How to Believe in Yourself', *BetterUp*, *https://www.betterup.com/blog/how-to-believe-yourself*

Fingerprint for Success, fingerprintforsuccess.com

Easy Generator, easygenerator.com

Psychology Compass, *https://psychologycompass.com/*

Bose, R., *Medium*, medium.com

Chandler, S., *Hinge Marketing*, hingemarketing.com

'Keeping Your Word at Work', *MindTools*, https://www.mindtools.com/awtninu/keeping-yourword-at-work

'You Can't Change the People You Work With, So Do This Instead', *ThinkAdvisor*, 4 February 2021, https://www.thinkadvisor.com/2021/02/04/you-cantchange-the-people-you-work-with-so-do-this-instead/

Scan QR code to access the
Penguin Random House India website